INTERNATIONAL GUIDE TO FORMS OF ADDRESS

INTERNATIONAL GUIDE TO FORMS OF ADDRESS

Compiled and written by

T. L. Shanson

MACMILLAN

First published in 1997 by Macmillan

an imprint of Macmillan Publishers Ltd
25 Eccleston Place, London SW1W 9NF
and Basingstoke

Associated companies throughout the world

ISBN 0 333 662970

1 3 5 7 9 8 6 4 2

A CIP catalogue record for this book is available from
the British Library.

Typeset by CentraCet, Cambridge
Printed and bound in Great Britain by
Mackays of Chatham plc, Chatham, Kent

CONTENTS

INDEX OF COUNTRIES
AND TERRITORIES

Gabon
Gambia (The)
Georgia
Germany
Ghana
Gibraltar
Great Britain (see
   United Kingdom)
Greece
Greenland (see
   Denmark)
Grenada
Grenadines (see Eastern
   Caribbean States)
Guadaloupe
Guam and the
   Marianas
Guatemala
Guiana, French
Guinea
Guinea-Bissau
Guyana
Haiti
Honduras
Hong Kong
Hungary
Iceland
India
Indonesia
Iran
Iraq
Ireland
Ivory Coast (see Côte
   d'Ivoire)
Israel
Italy
Jamaica
Japan
Java (see Indonesia)
Jordan

Kazakhstan
Kenya
Kirghyzia
Kiribati
Korea, North
Korea, South
Kuwait
Laos
Latvia
Lebanon
Leeward Islands
   (see Polynesia,
   French)
Lesotho
Liberia
Libya
Liechtenstein
Lithuania
Luxembourg
Macao
Macedonia
Madagascar
Malawi
Malaysia
Maldives
Mali
Malta
Marshall Islands
Martinique
Mauritania
Mauritius
Mexico
Micronesia
Moldova
Monaco
Mongolia
Montserrat (see Eastern
   Caribbean States)
Morocco
Mozambique

Myanmar (see Burma)
Namibia
Nauru
Nepal
Netherlands
Netherlands Antilles
New Caledonia
New Zealand
Nicaragua
Niger
Nigeria
Norway
Oman
Pakistan
Palau (Belau)
Panama
Papua New Guinea
Paraguay
Peru
Philippines
Pitcairn Island
Poland
Polynesia, French
Portugal
Principe (see São
   Tomé)
Puerto Rico
Qatar
Quebec (see Canada)
Ras Al-Khaimah (see
   United Arab
   Emirates)
Réunion
Romania
Russia
Rwanda
Saba (see Netherlands
   Antilles)
San Marino
São Tomé & Principe

Saudi Arabia
Senegal
Serbia and Montenegro
(see Yugoslavia)
Seychelles
Sharja (see United Arab
Emiratos)
Sierre Leone
Singapore
Slovak Republic
Slovenia
Solomon Islands
Somalia
South Africa
South Georgia & South
Sandwich Islands
Spain
Sri Lanka
St Christopher (see
Eastern Caribbean
States)
St Eustatius (see
Netherlands Antilles)
St Helena
St Lucia (see Eastern
Caribbean States)
St Maartens (see
Netherlands Antilles
& French Polynesia)

St Nevis (see Eastern
Caribbean States)
St Vincent (see Eastern
Caribbean States)
Sudan
Suriname
Swaziland
Sweden
Switzerland
Syria
Tajikistan
Tahiti (see Polynesia,
French)
Taiwan
Tanzania & Zanzibar
Thailand
Tibet (see China)
Timor (see Indonesia)
Tobago (see Trinidad)
Togo
Tonga
Trinidad & Tobago
Tunisia
Turkey
Turkmenistan
Turks & Caicos Islands
Tuvalu
Uganda
Ukraine

Umm Al Qaiwan (see
United Arab
Emirates)
United Arab Emirates
United Kingdom
United States of
America
Uruguay
Uzbekistan
Vanuatu
Vatican
Venezuela
Vietnam
Virgin Islands,
American
Virgin Islands, British
Wallis & Fortuna
Western Sahara
Western Samoa and
American Samoa
Windward Islands
(see Polynesia,
French
Yemen
Yugoslavia (Serbia and
Montengro)
Zaïre
Zambia
Zanzibar (see Tanzania)
Zimbabwe

INTRODUCTION

It had never occurred to you. It is your first meeting and you are introduced to an important businessman. Impressions count. He presents his card, and you are faced with a name string, perhaps unpronounceable, without any clear clue as to whether the first name, last name, or fifth name in the string is his family name, or indeed whether you should address him by his family name or not. How on earth do you acknowledge him?

This book tells you.

There is no hard and fast principle to fall back on with worldwide forms of address, only guidelines. Each nation, and sometimes each community within the same nation, enjoys its individual traditions, conduct, and rules of courtesy. I consistently found during my research that different authorities, often citizens of the same country, held diverse views on what appear to be fairly simple issues about their country's social conduct.

Many countries enjoy traditions that are quite unique to them. This has made the task difficult and I have abandoned any inclination to try and impose a standard layout or universal approach.

The cardinal purpose of this work is to be a ready reference, to demystify and simplify the peculiarities of addressing someone correctly in distant countries, the ignorance of which so often gives unintended offence.

For those countries where English is in common use or where, for practical and business purposes, it is acceptable to use it, refer to the forms of address used in the country chapter on the United

Kingdom. This will usually be sufficient for salutations and introductions between ordinary citizens. Where other forms of address apply, such as for persons of prominence, and even eminence, I provide further details under the relevant country chapters.

Readers mystified by Arab names will find a separate chapter explaining their name structures and forms of address. Few Arab countries conform to a general rule, so the country chapters will clarify national traits in greater detail.

This is not intended to be an academic study, and I have avoided using linguistic jargon as far as possible, resorting to technical terms only where clarity demanded them. In many countries with naming customs similar to those of the UK or USA, terms such as *given name*, *first name*, and *forename* (or *surname* and *family name*) may be used interchangeably, and in those cases no fine distinctions are implied by my use of one term over another. Where there is an important distinction to be drawn (for instance where a given name comes last, rather than first, in the sequence) this is made clear in the text. Many countries, of course, have no such concepts in their naming systems.

I am primarily concerned in this work with correct forms of address between ordinary members of society, simply because most businessmen and travellers mix more with ordinary people than with those in exalted positions. However, I have not neglected the mighty, and report quite extensively on correct forms of address for people in important posts or with titles of nobility.

Each chapter therefore runs in reverse order of celebrity. That is to say, they first explain how to greet and address the commoner, and thereafter persons of position, usually in ascending order. This is not meant to offend those with titles and position, but is designed to be a practical way to present at the top of each chapter the terms most often needed by our readers for easy reference.

These pages are abundant with curiosities. Some countries have customs that seem decidedly quirky to the English speaker. There is the delightful greeting in Papua New Guinea of *Big Man*, for instance, which is used to address a chief. Many countries possess no equivalent of a family name or surname, resulting in somewhat of an identity crisis for Westerners. Indonesians tend not to have family names, and in Bali the order of names may change to mislead evil spirits. Which name do you use?

I have tried not to be straight-laced all of the time, but decided (reluctantly) not to include such colloquial gems as that chirpy but cheeky Singapore greeting, "Eh Goondoo" (akin to "wotcher buffoon"). I have no wish for my readers to be assaulted.

The award for simplicity must go to Israel, where it is difficult to insult even the most exalted personality by an inarticulate honorific. Expressed another way, you can probably insult everyone with impunity. Israel is exceptional. Most countries take their forms of address very seriously, and several nationalities may be inclined to take to the sword at the drop of a pronoun.

There are countries such as Malaysia, using what the unaccustomed may regard as an exotic formula for addressing those who are Malays, often using one of the middle names, with yet another way to address those who are Chinese, who use their first names as surnames and the two following names as compound forenames. The Indian community in Malaysia is different again. Other multi-cultural communities, such as those of Namibia, where they speak more than 11 languages or dialects, are just as complex. In Thailand, for instance, you address someone by their first name, though their family name comes last and is used only in written forms of address or on formal occasions. Conversely, in neighbouring Cambodia, the custom is transposed, as in Vietnam. For real confusion, try Iceland, or Burma.

Asian countries in particular subscribe to customs that treasure honour and position, measured, for example, by the way one presents a visiting card as well as by oral forms of address. Even in the United States there are many customs that tend to be overlooked or which many foreigners are simply not aware of that will mark you as knowledgeable when you read this, and use them correctly.

This work of reference is designed to equip you with that competence worldwide.

ACKNOWLEDGEMENTS

I am indebted to Dr George Philip of the LSE who acted as consultant for feminine forms of address in Latin American countries, and to Dr David Matthews of SOAS for his invaluable counsel on Muslim Indian names. Any errors which remain are of course, my own. This is a new project, and the first international guide to forms of address and names to be published: it will no doubt be possible to make improvements in future editions, and suggestions from readers will be welcome.

NOTE

The word *honorific* has been used throughout the book to mean an ordinary title (equivalent to the English *Mr*, *Ms*, *Miss*, or *Mrs*). The term *courtesy title* here has the restricted meaning of a professional title (such as *Dr* in English or *Licenciado* in Spanish) as distinct from the standard honorific.

ARAB NAMES &
FORMS OF ADDRESS

[We recognise that it is irritating to turn back to this chapter every time you refer to an entry for a specific Arab country. We have therefore condensed relevant portions and inserted them into the appropriate chapters. The full text appears below.]

There are no hard and fast rules with Arab names. Everything is loose and variable, and different influences govern the practices of each Arab country.

Although translations and pronunciations will vary with each country, in general, the Arab equivalents of Mr, Mrs, and Miss are: Sayid, Sayeda, and Anissa respectively.

Within the string of Arab names everyone usually has their own given name followed by their father's given name. Thus: *Mohamad Jemal or Mohamad bin Jemal* (where *bin* means "son of"). Sometimes, mostly in Saudi Arabia, Iraq, and the Gulf States, ibn is used instead of bin, but means exactly the same. Complications arise as the string is added to by the practice of honouring ancestors.

Women also derive their names from their father, and sometimes add their father's father, and so on, ending with their family name. They retain their names after marriage, so they do not take their husband's name.

The use of the full name chain that many Arabs use is for official use on documentation only, for example, for passports and marriage certificates. Otherwise, it is not necessary to refer to them all.

In general, *Abu* appearing in the name string of a married man indicates that he is the father of a child of the name following. Thus

Abu Jamil shows that he is the father of Jamil. Similarly, the name following the word *Umm* in a woman's name string indicates that she is the mother of that child, as with *Umm Ismat* (mother of Ismat).

In correspondence the rules are again variable. Use their business card as a clue.

Some surnames are derived from tribes as a matter of family policy. The root name (i.e. the last name) is often a description of ancestors, a tribal name, or a place.

Example of the derivation of the name string of a male, Ali Abdullah Mughram Al-Ghamdi:

Given name	Father's name	Grandfather's name	Surname, perhaps tribal name
Ali	Abdullah	Mughram	Al-Ghamdi

In the following example of an *Egyptian* name (see Egypt chapter),
Abdel Aziz / Saleh Eddin / Abdel Aziz,
(NB: this name reads as Abdel Aziz Saleh Eddin Abdel Aziz)
Abdel Aziz together comprise the first name, Saleh Eddin is the father's name, and Abdel Aziz might be the family name but could also be the grandfather's name.

Note that the pronouns "Al" and "El" (tribe of) that often precede the final name are used less as you move away from the Gulf.

So you will tend always to find a person's given name and always the name of their father, frequently also their grandfather's name, then their tribal-type name, which often, but not always, is preceded by "Al".

The same principle applies to men and to women.

In oral address all that matters will depend entirely on the relationship between the parties.

Again, the custom varies in different countries, but in general people do not call someone only by their first names except between close social friends. They will always use the honorific before the given name when addressing each other at work. Thus, using the example of the first name string above, he would be addressed simply as *Mr Ali*.

However, there are Arab countries where, as a general term of address, you may use the first name only (whether male or female), provided you are on familiar terms and you have been told to do so.

In correspondence it is usual, but not the rule, to use the honorific followed by the given name, father's name, and last name. Thus: *Sayid Ali Abdullah Al-Ghamdi*. Therefore, if any names are to be left out, they should be those sandwiched between the father's name and the final name in the string.

In our example, the Al-Ghamdi will be carried forward to the next generation so will always remain the final name in the string.

With both the male and female lines, some families decide to call it quits after a finite number of names, bringing a halt to the chain. But they will always name the father (the second name in the chain).

In countries such as Egypt, Syria, Jordan, and Lebanon, family names are often translations of occupations. This particularly happens in the older cultures where Western traditions have had limited influence. Thus: *Al-Naggar* (carpenter).

It is becoming a familiar practice in some Arab countries to tag on yet another family name after the tribal or other end-name to indicate a family has decided to call a halt to the continuation of the name string. This annexation becomes a permanent surname.

In this example of name mutation, the middle portion is sometimes contracted into one word. Thus the middle names in Mostafa *Abd El Latif* Nofal become Abdulatif.

There is often no way to distinguish between a married and an unmarried woman by their names.

When corresponding with a married woman it is customary with many households to do so via the husband. Different Arab countries apply different formulas to this and apply different traditions to determine a woman's provenance by the names.

A single woman whose name is Taibah Atallah El-Garny would be addressed informally (and orally) by acquaintances as *Miss Taibah*, but formally as *Miss El-Garny*.

In correspondence she would be addressed as *Miss Taibah El-Garny*.

By way of explanation *Mrs Rawia M.M. El-Garny*'s name (Egyptian in this example), is derived as follows:

The first name is the given name, then her father's and grandfather's initials (men can use initials for these names too), then her family name (El-Garny).

She would probably be addressed orally as *Mrs Rawia*. Remember there are no firm rules, just probabilities. Never call her just "Rawia". In correspondence write: Dear Mrs Rawia El-Garny, *not* Dear Mrs El-Garny.

However, if you are addressing an Arab in a Western country you might well be expected to employ Western custom. You would therefore greet her as Mrs El-Garny, and our earlier example would become Mr Al-Ghamdi.

Readers should remember that it is far more important to be aware of social customs than correct forms of address if one is to avoid giving offence. Addressing someone by the wrong name is excusable, but pointing the sole of one's foot when sitting cross-legged, touching someone, or being familiar with a woman in stricter Arab societies, are not.

Titles

Titles are very important. Therefore in correspondence address an engineer as: *Engineer Ali Al-Ghamdi*. This also applies to lawyers and doctors. Sometimes it may be stretched to include accountants and architects, but there is no firm rule.

In oral address too, use the full name with professional title. On subsequent mention one should say simply "Engineer", or "Doctor", etc.

Military titles are also very important and should always be used.

Arab countries employ a variety of titles to designate members of their royal and ruling families. *Emir* and *Sultan* are the preferred Royal titles. There is also the salutation *Effendi* (Turkish derivative), and such religious appellations as *Imam* (religious teacher). *Sheikh* (pronounced like the English word *shake*, but with a guttural gurgle for the *kh*) is tribal. The word sheikh, meaning "old man", is an honorific used among the tribes to describe a tribal leader or man of widely accepted distinction. In the UAE, sheikh applies to the rulers and leading members of the rulers' families.

RECOGNISING INDIAN
NAME STRUCTURES

Below is some guidance on understanding name construction used for and by Indian communities wherever they might be, and its significance on forms of address.

The Indian community is divided religiously between Hindus, Muslims, Sikhs, Parses, Christians, Jains, etc, so it is natural that some of those communities will be addressed differently. We are focusing on the most likely issues. There are also regional groups, such as Tamils, though Tamil is not a religion, but an ethnic community with its own language. The caste system in India has no significant impact on forms of address.

Except for the Muslim Indian community Western forms of address should be used. Thus: Mr Thiagarajah THIRUNAGAN (Hindu).

Tamil Hindus

Tamil Hindus in particular have long forenames which are often abbreviated, and the shortened form is acceptable in both written and oral usage. Thus *Subramaniam Damodara Pakirisamy* is shortened to *Mr S. D. P. Samy*, where the application of the final initial *P* is deliberate and indicates that *Samy* is truncated. Others may elect to shorten their name differently – see examples below.

Some examples of name reconstruction (some of which are exceptions to the 'rules' above).

Gnaguru s/o Thamboo Mylvaganam	=	M. G. Guru
Kanapathi Pillai Nirumdan	=	K. P. Niru

M. Padmanathan Seethapathy	=	S. Nathan
Mangalam Amaladaj	=	M. Daj
Murugiah Rajahram	=	Muru
Nataragam Kumararajah	–	N. K. Rajah
Murugasu Puvanendran	=	M. Puva
Sivanatha Sivagnanaratnum	=	S. S. Ratnam

Muslims

With Indian Muslim names there is no concept of a surname. There are usually three elements to a man's name and some women's names, and a man or woman may be addressed by any of them that the person concerned chooses to be identified with – it is really a matter of personal preference.

It is a confusing concept for Westerners to appreciate, but sons or daughters could take completely different names, as might brothers and sisters.

With, for instance, *Jamil Akhtar Khan*, Jamil is Arabic for *beautiful*, and Akhtar is Persian for *star*, Khan is tribal.

Names often indicate one's ancestral region. Someone with the last name *Khan* is likely to have Pathan ancestors from Afghanistan, though there are many areas in India where a person called *Khan* may have settled.

The honorific to employ (orally and in correspondence) is *Sahib* (meaning *possessor* in Arabic), spoken or written after the chosen name. *Sahib* may be masculine or feminine, though *Sahiba* is often employed instead when addressing women. Thus: *Jamil Sahib*.

Alternatively use *Begum* (Madam) when referring to a married woman, or when introducing your own wife, but say *Begum Sahiba* when addressing the married lady in question. It is used either after or before the preferred name. In the Punjab the use of Begum is preferred to Sahib/a.

The Hindi honorific *Ji* is also understood and widely used (see chapter on India). Similarly, filial terms are often employed, as with the use of āpä (elder sister) after the name.

Muslim Indians speak Urdu, and it is common practice for them to take pen names, known as *takhallus*. These are acquired for the purpose of self-image when writing poetry, which is apparently a national trait. Thus with the name *Aqil Ahmad Danish*, Danish is the pen name (or poetic surname, meaning knowledgeable and wise), replacing his original last name (though it need not) and is sufficiently acceptable in society for it to appear as the name in the telephone directory. In this sense it effectively becomes a surname.

All names have meanings. The majority are from Arabic or Persian. Some names are chosen by parents for their child by opening the Koran to a page at random and selecting the first name that appears.

Some male Muslims have *Sayyid* or *Syed* as a name. This means he claims direct descendancy of the Holy Prophet. Many Shia Muslims claim descendancy from the Holy Prophet, but in general a person's names do not distinguish Shias and Sunnis.

Female names follow the same pattern in that they need not (though may) have a surname. A woman does not necessarily take her husband's name upon marriage, though she may elect to do so by choosing any one of them or his pen name.

Many of the above properties are common to Muslim communities in general, though the tradition of name giving varies from country to country, and local traditions have been influenced by other characteristics in many parts of the world. Muslim names in Indonesia, for instance, are far removed from classical pronunciation.

In general, though not necessarily for Indian Muslims, Abu added to the name of a married male indicates that he is the father of a child of the same name. Thus *Abu Jamil* shows that he is the father of *Jamil*. Similarly, *Ibn*, or *Bin* means *son of* (masculine).

The name of a child after the word *Umm* indicates that the subject is the mother of that child, as with *Umm Ismat* (mother of Ismat). *Bint* before a woman's name shows that she is the daughter of the name following, as with *Ismat Bint Chughatai* (Ismat, daughter of Chughatai).

Sikhs

Within the Sikh community every male has the name *Singh* (meaning Lion) after his given name. Thus: *Ranjit Singh Gill*. He will be addressed as *Bhai Ranjit Singh*, where *Bhai* means "brother".

Similarly, every female Sikh has the name *Kaur* (meaning "Princess") after her given name, which, too, may be followed by the surname. Thus: *Ranjit Kaur Dhillon*. She would be addressed as *Bibi Ranjit Kaur*, where *Bibi* means "sister". *Sardar* and *Sardarni* may be used instead of *Bhai* and *Bibi* respectively.

Therefore *Sardar / Bhai* are equivalent to *Mr*, and *Sadarni / Bibi* are equivalent to *Ms* or *Mrs*.

It is a foundation of the Sikh religion that all men and women are equally respected. Therefore Sikhs adopt common names – a tradition that extends to the richest and poorest alike. Thus an interesting feature of Sikh names is that both the male and female can have the same given name distinguished only by *Singh* or *Kaur*, as with *Daljit Singh Gill* and *Daljit Kaur Gill*.

Male children are addressed as *Kaka*, and female children as *Kaki*. Thus a family might comprise: *Sardar Beant Singh (father)*; *Sardar-nee Beant Kaur* (mother); *Kaka Beant Singh* (son); and *Kaki Beant Kaur* (daughter), where these first words are forms of address, not names.

The tradition is that once a Sikh is baptised, he or she becomes a *Khalsa*, whereupon all last names are renounced and the person should adopt *Singh* (m) or *Kaur* (f) as their last name. For instance, *Gobind Rai* (m) becomes *Gobind Singh* after becoming a *Khalsa*.

However, some people introduce Singh as a middle name out of common practice.

People often attach a third name to distinguish themselves from another person with the same first-name as their own. In India the name they attach is sometimes the name of their city or village and sometimes it is their surname. Thus: *Jarnail Singh Bhindrawale*, where *Bhindrawale* is the name of a village in Punjab, or *Manjit Singh Calcutta*, where Calcutta is the city he is from.

When a child is born into a Sikh family, most families introduce the name *Singh* as a middle name in the hope that the child will eventually become baptised. So, in most cases *Rajinder Singh Dhillon* would become *Rajinder Singh* after baptism, where *Dhillon* is a surname.

However, the name Singh is also used by the Rajputs, a warrior race from Northwest India who are Hindus, for their first-born son (e.g. *Rajiv Singh*). There is no parallel for the use of *Kaur* for the female Rajput.

A fairly common practice (though generally not used by those who have migrated to the West) is to insert *son of* or *daughter of* before the family name, expressed either as initials (see chapter on Malaysia) or in full. This is usually for formal documents only and is not used in oral forms of address, though they might be used when writing.

SPANISH AMERICAN FORMS OF ADDRESS – A CHA CHA AROUND THE FEMININE FORM

Identifying how to address women properly in these societies can be trickier than for men, who are dealt with in the respective country chapters. Here is a separate guide to the feminine gender puzzle.

Whilst every regional country retains its idiosyncrasies, if we are to recommend a generalisation of how to treat feminine forms of address, our treatment of Argentina is probably the best model for all of Spanish America.

In traditional Spanish American societies a woman would take her husband's name after marriage, but in addition to her own name rather than as a replacement. So if she were called Barbara Betancourt Perez at the time of her marriage to Sr Lopez, she would then become Barbara Betancourt Perez de Lopez (where *de* means "(wife) of"). The second surname (Perez) would not normally be referred to orally (unless her name were genuinely double-barrelled), but would exist on paper.

De usually signifies to whom a woman is married, but in some cases may be part of a pre-existing name.

However, these traditions are now changing. Many women no longer take their husbands' names at all. Professional women tend not to want to change their names upon marriage. The divorce and separation rate is now high among Latin America's urban middle classes, and women will not usually keep the name of a divorced husband. Others no longer feel obliged to adopt a particular convention and may keep or drop a name – for effect. It is, however, rare for a woman to drop her own surname altogether upon marriage.

Nevertheless, rather than simply following rules, the visitor is advised wherever possible to find out the name and preferred mode of address of a woman acquaintance.

Thus, if *Sr Díaz* married Srta *Gavier* and they had a daughter, she would be known as (say) *Magdalena Díaz Gavier*. In turn, when *Magdalena* marries *Sr Campora*, she would become *Magdelena Díaz Gavier de Campora*. If you are writing to her, and you don't know her, then use all the names (*Sra Díaz Gavier de Campora*).

Orally, one would normally address and refer to a married woman by her prefered surname, e.g. *Señora Campora* or *Señora de Campora*. For verbal communication, *Señora Díaz de Campora* is too long. The same applies to unmarried women. *Srta María García* is too long, so one would tend to say *Srta García* in conversation.

Orally, the second surname is not generally used, so you would probably refer to the lady as *Sra Díaz de Campora*. The problem sometimes arises that *Díaz Gavier* may turn out to be a double-barrelled name, in which case *Sra Díaz Gavier de Campora* would be correct. Fortunately, first name terms are often established early on. Younger people will adopt an informal mode of address quite quickly.

If people present their name card, or you know them better, it is best to ask for the preferred mode of address. Remember that some women don't use their married names at all.

It is worth noting that in general any woman university teacher will be addressed as *profesora*, as with American usage of professor; and the title *doctora* is often used for women lawyers as well as for doctors and those with PhDs. If in doubt, use *doctora* for any educated woman, as the term is never unflattering.

The use of Doña (f) (and Don for men) need not be formal – it can even be affectionate, especially if followed by a diminutive as in *doña Elsita*; however it is always a sign of respect reserved for people older than oneself. It is not generally used for women under about 50. Use *doctor(a)* instead.

Afghanistan

A confusing country for us to begin with. Some people have surnames, and some do not. Some have only one name. There is no easy formula for the foreigner to engage.

In general, there is no equivalent to a surname and one should address someone by their first name, thus Dr Hashmatullah Mojadidi would be Dr Hashmatullah, but in formal situations he should be addressed with the full name, as Dr Hashmatullah Mojadidi.

With others, an entirely different practice may prevail. For Dr Mohammad Shafi Zafar, for instance, it would be acceptable to address him as Dr Zafar, or by all three names. Unfortunately, those unfamiliar with local name characteristics will not be able to tell which policy to employ.

People without surnames usually use their father's name after their given name, and are addressed, as above, as Mr Firstname.

In correspondence one usually uses all names.

Upon marriage, women generally do not adopt their husband's name.

Albania

Zoti AGRON LEKA

The last name is the family name.

$$\text{Mr} = Zoti \qquad \text{Mrs} = Zonja \qquad \text{Miss} = Zonjusha$$

For general purposes address people, whether writing or orally, by the honorific and both names. Thus: Zoti Agron Leka.

In formal situations you should always use both names, but less formally you may use the honorific with the given name. Thus: Zoti Agron. Friends use the first name without the honorific. Thus: Agron.

The same applies whether addressing men or women.

Algeria

Monsieur ALI Lakhdari

The official language is Arabic but there is an important influence from the French language. French is widely used in administrative circles, but Arabic is used by Parliament and at local council level. Companies generally use French.

WHEN USING FRENCH:

Spoken:
$$\text{Mr} = Monsieur \qquad \text{Mrs} = Madame \qquad \text{Miss} = Mademoiselle$$

In correspondence abbreviate to:

M.   Mme.   *Melle.*

In Algeria the abbreviation *Mr.* is frequently used instead of *M.*, though it is incorrect usage to do so.

   Mr = *Sayed*   Mrs = *Sayeda*   Miss = *Anisa* (with one S)

Informally, and as a friendly gesture, one says *Khuya* (brother) or *Khti* (sister). These introductions stand alone – do not say their name. In England, it would be the equivalent, for instance, of saying "Hi Mike". Similarly, when appropriate you can say *Anme* (my father's brother) or *Khalti* (my mother's sister), but use them only when addressing older people.

Unlike Tunisia, which otherwise shares its linguistic diversity, names in Algeria do not possess lengthy ancestral name strings. However, there are many people with the name prefix *Ben* (meaning *son of*), but it is a formal part of the surname (or family name), as with *Bendjama*. Remember that the family name is always first and the given name(s) always follow.

Women take their husband's family name instead upon marriage. The feminine equivalent of the name prefix *Ben* is *Bent* (meaning daughter of), but *Bent* is rarely used, and *Ben* is more usual in women's names. Again, this is common but not universal.

In correspondence the family name appears first, followed by given name(s). Thus: Monsieur HAMDAN Hassan, where Hamdan is the family name. Similarly, it will be Madame Hamdan and Melle. Hamdan (Miss).

Formal invitations are addressed to Mr/Mrs *Family Name* then *Given Name*.

Unlike in Morocco, the name order is not reversed for oral communication.

Sheikh (plus both names) is said when addressing religious chiefs. Sometimes people speak colloquially of their fathers as Sheikh.

There are no special forms of address for those with professions or qualifications except for lawyers, who are addressed as *Maître*, and doctors.

There are some variant titles used in Western Algeria, where there is still some Spanish influence, but they are not in common usage.

Instead of saying *Sir*, Algerians say *Si*. Thus: Si Mohammed. It is an informal form of respect. There is no feminine equivalent.

Caution: Morocco uses *Lalla* as a feminine form of address for those with status, but in Algeria *Lalla* is (supposed to be) a term of endearment used by a daughter-in-law when addressing her mother-in-law.

Andorra

Catalan is the official language. French and Spanish are widely spoken.

Catalan forms of address need only be used when addressing government officials for formal situations, so are generally not required by foreigners. For practical purposes use either French or Spanish forms of address in the same way as they would be used in those countries.

WHEN USING SPANISH:

Mr = *Señor*   Mrs = *Señora*   Miss = *Señorita*

WHEN USING FRENCH:

Mr = *Monsieur*   Mrs = *Madame*   Miss = *Mademoiselle*

Angola

Senhor José António KIALA

PORTUGUESE IS SPOKEN.

Mr = *Senhor*   Mrs = *Senhora*   Miss = *Menina*

In correspondence abbreviate to:

Sr.   *Sra.* (Senhorita is rarely used)

The family name appears after the given names. Thus: José António Kiala is addressed orally as Senhor Kiala.

In writing he would be addressed by his first and family names, thus: Senhor José Kiala.

Women are usually addressed orally as *Senhora family name*, but in correspondence one may optionally address her as *Dona*, but only by using the initial D. Thus: *D. Filamina Kiala*. Remember that *Dona* should not be used in unabbreviated form when writing and if using *Senhora*, abbreviate to Sra.

Forms of address for people with professions:

Senhor(a) Doutor(a)
Senhor(a) Engenheiro (Engenheira)

Oral forms for officials:

Sua Excelência Senhor Ministro (when talking *about* The Minister)
Ilustre Senhor . . . etc. (when talking *to* The Minister)

When writing, open (for persons with rank and position) with:

Excelentíssimo Senhor Excelentíssima Senhora
Prezado Senhor / Prezada Senhora

Caro Senhor / Cara Senhora
Ilustre Senhor / Ilustre Senhora

and sign off:

Subscrevo-me atenciosamente (Yours Faithfully)
Cordiais saudações (Yours Sincerely)

Antigua & Barbuda

Mr James THOMAS

English is spoken and forms of address correspond to those used in the UK.

Argentina

Señora Magdalena Díaz Gavier *de CÁMPORA*

(See also the general entry on Spanish-American forms of address)

Spanish is spoken.

Mr = *Señor*   Mrs = *Señora*   Miss = *Señorita*

In correspondence abbreviate to:

Sr.   Sra.   Srta.

The given name is followed by the father's surname, then (sometimes, so not necessarily) the mother's surname.

Married women use Señora followed by the given name, father's surname, "de" (of), then their husband's surname. Thus: Señora

María García de Domínguez. Write to her by her full name, but say (formally) Señora de Dominguez. (Señora Dominguez is equally correct and probably more usual, as it's shorter). When acquainted, address her less formally by saying Señora María.

Luisa López, an unmarried woman, would be addressed orally as Señorita López, and in writing as Srta. Lopez.

It is customary to refer to professional people by their qualification. Someone with a degree in engineering is called Ingeniero (m) or Ingeniera (f), and someone with a university degree in any subject is a Licenciado (m) or Licenciada (f). A medical doctor or person with a doctorate in any discipline is a Doctor (m) or Doctora (f). In oral address use the professional title followed by the father's surname.

Licenciado and Doctor are not preceded by Señor, but other professional titles are, in speaking and in writing.

Title	Spoken form (m/f)	In correspondence (m/f)
Doctor	Doctor/Doctora	Dr./Dra.
Ingeniero (engineer)	Señor Ingeniero/Señora Ingeniera	Ing.
Profesor	Señor Profesor/Señora Profesora	Prof.
Arquitecto (architect)	Señor Arquitecto/Señora Arquitecta	Arquitecto/ Arquitecta

When writing, use Ing., Lic., Dr., respectively, but follow the professional title by the given name, then the father's surname (then sometimes, though not necessarily, the mother's surname).

There are neither hereditary nor conferred titles.

The formal opening and signing off of letters to persons of rank and position are:

De mi mayor consideración / Le saluda atentamente

The use of Don/Doña with the given name is a polite way to refer to a person older than 50, although it is not frequently used these days. Do not place the honorific before Don/Doña. A respectful, but less formal mode of address is Doctor/a.

An ambassador is addressed as "Embajador", and a Minister as "Ministro".

Armenia

Paron Zorab MNATSAKANIAN

Armenians are trying to distance themselves from the patronymic system, a memento of Russian rule. Instead, most people are now adopting conventional Western forms of address, with the family name appearing last. Thus: Zorab MNATSAKANIAN.

Some older people might retain their patronymic, usually by adding an "itch" to their father's name (Thus: Zorab Ivanovitch).

We are advised that almost all Armenian names are readily identifiable because they end with -ian, as with Sarkissian, or in some cases -iants.

Mr = *Paron*   Mrs = *Teekeen*   Miss = *Oriort*

Married women do not take their husband's family name after marriage.

There are no titles.

Australia

Mr R. J. SMITH

Apply traditional English forms of address, Mr, Mrs, Miss, and Ms.

Apart from the lapse of the use of *Esquire* in correspondence, all else is very much the same as the UK.

There is a growing preference for women to use Ms instead of Miss or Mrs. *Ms* is apparently now always used within the federal civil service.

Titles are no longer bestowed and are largely gone.

Political Forms of Address

The Upper House of the Federal Parliament is the House of Senate, and its members are addressed orally as Senators. They may be introduced, for example, as Senator Frank Fine or Senator Fine, using family and/or all names. In correspondence open with Dear Sir (if formal) or Dear Senator (less formal).

The Lower House of the Federal Parliament is the House of Representatives, which is the more important chamber and mirrors the British House of Commons. Its members are addressed orally without distinction using the casual honorific Mr, Mrs/Miss/Ms. In correspondence open with Dear Sir/Madam (if formal) or Dear Mr/ etc. (if informal).

State Parliaments are bicameral (with two Houses of Parliament) except for Queensland, which has abolished its Upper House. In some states the Lower House is known as the Legislative Assembly, and its members are addressed orally as Mr or Mrs/Miss/Ms. In correspondence open with Dear Sir/Madam (formal) or with Dear

Mr/etc. (less formal). Members are entitled to have the suffix MLA (Member of the Legislative Assembly) after their names. However, in South Australia and Tasmania the legislative chamber is called the House of Assembly; its members are addressed the same way though there is no suffix applied to names.

State Upper Houses are known as Legislative Councils, and their members are addressed orally with the casual honorific Mr or Mrs/Miss/Ms. However, they should be introduced with formality as The Honourable (all names), Member of the Legislative Council. In correspondence they should be addressed with their names suffixed with the initials MLC. Open correspondence with Dear Sir/Madam (if formal) or Dear Mr/Mrs etc (if informal).

The British Queen is represented by a Governor-General, who is addressed orally and in writing by that title. There are also six State Governors, who are each addressed as Your Excellency (His Excellency if by introduction), thereafter as Sir/Madam, or informally thereafter as Mr/Mrs etc. In correspondence open with Your Excellency (formal) or Dear Mr Governor (informal).

The only persons entitled to be addressed as Right Honourable are members of the Privy Council, who chiefly comprise Governors-General, Prime Ministers, senior Federal Ministers, and Justices of the High Court. Certain Lord Mayors (where the honour attaches to the office, not the person) are also so entitled for the duration of their office. Except for the Mayors, the entitlement is for life. Only Privy Councillors who are also Peers may post the initials PC after their names.

The right to be addressed with the title The Honourable belongs to the President of the Senate, Speaker of the House of Representatives, members of the Commonwealth Judiciary, Ministers of State Government, Presidents and Members of Legislative Councils, Speakers of Legislative Assemblies, Chief Justices and Puisne Judges of the State Supreme Courts, and the President and Judges of the

New South Wales Court of Appeal. Upon retirement only the following are permitted to continue to use the title: Ministers of State Government who have served at least one year as Premier or three years as a Minister; Presidents of the House of Senate and State Legislative Councils, Speakers of the House of Representatives, and State Legislative Assemblies who have served three years in office; Members of the Legislative Council with continuous service of not less than ten years.

Some Members of Commonwealth and State judiciaries are also entitled to lifetime use of the title, provided they have been formally sanctioned to do so.

Aboriginals are usually addressed in the same way as other Australian citizens, but there is now a preference by some to be referred to as members of a clan instead of a tribe, and their attitude towards correct forms of address is under revision. What this means is unclear. For practical purposes there is, as yet, no different form of address.

Austria

Herr Dr. Walter F. MAGRUTSCH

Ordinary citizens are addressed, both orally and in writing, as:

Mr = *Herr*   Mrs and Ms = *Frau*   Miss = *Fräulein*

followed by the family name.

Women are addressed as *Frau*, not Fräulein, once they have reached 18 years. Thus: *Frau Renate Brautigam*.

Academic & professional degrees: Use *Magister* (abbreviate to *Mag.* in correspondence) before the family name of someone with an academic degree, whether at bachelor or master level, but place *Herr* or *Frau* beforehand, thus (orally): Herr Magister Magrutsch. *Doctor/Doktor* is used for someone with a medical qualification, and for those with a PhD.

Place the occupational title between the honorific and professional title. Thus: *Herr Botschafter* (ambassador) *Dr. Magrutsch*.

Other examples of an honour string:
Herr General Sekretär (Mr General Secretary) Dr. Magrutsch
Herr Direktor (General Manager) Dr. Magrutsch

Aristocratic titles have been abolished under the Constitution, though in spoken language they might still be used.

Austrian titles may be written in English, though "Graf" (also used for Count) and "Gräfin" (Countess) are usually written in German. Graf is sometimes abbreviated to *Gf.* and Freiherr to *Frh.*

The title is followed by the family name in correspondence, but as an oral form of address the title is used alone (do not say the family name).

Title	In German	Address as
Archduke	Erzherzog	Kaiserliche Hoheit
Archduchess	Erzherzogin	Kaiserliche Hoheit (Imperial Highness)
Duke / Duchess	Herzog / Herzogin	Hoheit
Prince / Princess	Fürst / Fürstin	Durchlaucht
Count / Countess	Graf / Gräfin	Graf / Gräfin
Baron / Baroness	Baron / Baronin	Baron / Baronin
–	Baroness	Baroness

(NB: A Baroness is the unmarried daughter of a Baron)

Such titles as: Chevalier, Ritter, Cavaliere, etc apply to minor nobility but are no longer used conversationally. Instead, the preposition *von* (of) is inserted between the given and family names.

The Austrian President is addressed as "Sehr geehrter Herr Bundes-präsident (Dear Mr President), whilst the Chancellor is referred to as "Sehr geehrter Herr Bundeskanzler".

Azerbaijan

Janab Ismail Araz ogly MAMEDOV

Forms of address correspond to those used in Russia in that a patronymic system is used. It is preferable to use Azeri honorifics, although both Azeri and Russian will be understandable.

Azerbaijan enjoys distinctive differences from the Russian patro-nymic model, which in practice places Azeri forms of address closer to the Turkic system. The government plans to implement changes to encourage the use of Turkic forms of address on formal documents, such as passports. However, there is official resistance but popular support for the concept of using *Bei* instead of *Janab* (see below).

88% of the population are Muslim and 83% are Azeris. Armenians and others account for the balance.

WHEN USING AZERI:

$Mr = Janab$ $Mrs / Miss = Khanym$

WHEN USING RUSSIAN:

$Mr = Gospodin$ Mrs / Miss = Gospozha

There is no distinction between married and unmarried women.

The forename comes first, then the patronymic which shows filiation to the father, then the surname, which is passed on down the generations. Thus: *Ismail Araz ogly Mamedov* (m) where *ogly* is "*son of*" would be addressed as *Janab Mamedov*.

If we refer to *Fatimah Araz gyzy Mamedova* (f), note that *gyzy* means "daughter of", and there is a feminine ending of the family name (Mamedova). She is *Khanym Mamedova*.

The Russian patronymic is formed by adding "son of" or "daughter of" to the father's name, save that in Azerbaijan this is usually represented by the insertion of the Azeri word for *son of or daughter of*.

Using the Turkic formula, *Ismail Araz ogly Mamedov* will be known as *Ismail Araz ogly Mamedli*. Names ending with *ov* and *ev* will probably then end with *li* and *ly* respectively.

Some people are now adopting this system and introduce themselves, for example, as *Janab Mamedli*. Many do not.

Innumerable Azeri names end with *ov* or *ev* (masculine; *ova* or *eva* if feminine), except that there are special exceptions, such as *Mamedli* (a surname with the *li* ending), which is gender neutral. Similarly, names ending in *-zade* are neutral (as with *Mamedzade* or *Mamed-Zade*).

Whilst the honorifics *Janab* and *Khanym* precede the family name, sometimes *Bei* (an Azeri word of Turkic derivation) is used instead after the first name. Thus: *Ismail Bei*. Women can also apply this formula by placing *Khanym* after their first name. Therefore women may be addressed with *Khanym* before their family name, or after their first name. Oral and written forms of address are the same.

The use of Comrade as a form of address is now a relic superseded by Your Excellency, to be used when addressing high functionaries.

Although there are Islamic religious leaders, who might even be Mullahs, there is no extraordinary form of address for them, though religious leaders in general are often addressed as *Sheikh* before the family name, before the first name, or before all names.

In the religious world, male Muslims who have been to Mecca use *Hadjy* before their family name or after their first name. Women do not.

Bahamas

Miss Judith FRANCIS

Forms of address in the Bahamas are the same as for the UK, and honours are bestowed in the same way.

Members of Parliament are therefore referred to as Honourable Members, as in: Mr Arthur Jackson, The Honourable Member for . . .

Bahrein

Sayid KARIM Yousif AL ASFOOR

See also the chapter on Arab names.

There are no hard and fast rules.

Within the string of Arab names everyone usually has their own given name followed by their father's given name: Thus: Mohamad Jemal or Mohamad bin Jemal (where *bin* = son of). Complications arise as the string is added to by the practice of honouring ancestors.

Women also derive their names from their father, and sometimes add their father's father, and so on, ending with their family name. They retain their names after marriage, so they do not take their husband's name.

The full name chain that many Arabs have is for official use on documentation only, for example, for passports and marriage certificates. Otherwise, it is not necessary to refer to them all.

In correspondence the rules are again variable. Use their business card as a clue.

Some surnames are derived from tribes as a matter of family policy. The root name (i.e. the last name) is often a description of ancestors, a tribal name, or a place.

Example of the derivation of the name string of a male, Ali Abdullah Mughram Al-Ghamdi:

Given name	Father's name	Grandfather's name	Surname, perhaps tribal name
Ali	Abdullah	Mughram	Al-Ghamdi

So you will tend always to find a person's given name and always the name of their father, frequently also their grandfather's name, then their tribal-type name, which often, but not always, is preceded by "Al".

The same principle applies to men and to women.

In oral address all that matters will depend entirely on the relationship between the parties.

In general people do not call someone only by their first names except between close social friends. They will always use the honorific before the given name when addressing each other at work. Thus, using the example of the name string above, he would be addressed simply as *Mr Ali*.

In correspondence it is usual, but not the rule, to use the honorific followed by the given name, father's name, and last name. Thus: Mr Ali Abdullah Al-Ghamdi. Therefore, if any names are to be left out, they should be those sandwiched between the father's name and the final name in the string.

In our example, the Al-Ghamdi will be carried forward to the next generation, so will always remain the final name in the string.

Titles are very important. Therefore in correspondence address an engineer as: *Engineer Ali Al-Ghamdi*. This also applies to lawyers and doctors. Sometimes it may be stretched to include accountants and architects, but there is no firm rule.

In oral address too, use the full professional title. On subsequent mention one should say simply "Engineer", or "Doctor", etc.

There is often no way to distinguish between a married and an unmarried woman by their names.

There are no firm rules, just probabilities, but when corresponding to a married woman it is customary with many households to do so via the husband.

A single woman whose name, for example, is Taibah Atallah El-Garny would be addressed informally (and orally) by acquaintances as Miss Taibah, but formally as *Miss El-Garny*. In correspondence she would be addressed as *Miss Taibah El-Garny*.

The word *Sheikh* (pronounced like *shake*, but with a gargle on the kh), meaning "old man", is an honorific used among the tribes to describe a tribal leader or man of widely accepted distinction.

Military titles are very important and should always be used.

There is no set rule for spelling this, but *Abd*, *Abed* and *Abda* in the name refers to "of God". In this example: Mostafa Abd El Latif

Nofal, the middle portion is sometimes contracted into one word, thus: Abdulatif.

Bangladesh

Janab Anwar HUSSAIN

There are no hard and fast rules on the order of names. Muslims do not use family names, but other communities do. However, a section of the Muslim community "adopts" a family name, and in most cases people are known by their last name, following the usual Western style. Thus: Abdul KADER.

Oral and written forms of address among the business community usually correspond to those used in the UK.

In the vernacular the name of a Muslim is either preceded by *Janab* (for men), or *Begum* (for married women), or followed by *Shaheb* (for men). There is no specific form of address for an unmarried Muslim woman.

(Note: The use of *Sheikh* in the Arab context is considered a feudal relic and is no longer applied. However, there are people with *Sheikh* in their name string, such as prime minister Sheikh Hasina Wajid. It is used as a personal name, not a title.)

A Hindu name is either preceded by *Sri* (for men) or *Srimati* (for married women) or followed by *Babu* (for men). An unmarried woman is addressed as *Kumari* (followed by last name). Hindus also use Sahib to address professional people (e.g. Doctor Sahib).

There are conferred and hereditary titles which may either precede or follow the names. There are no firm rules.

A person with a professional degree is addressed by preceding the name with the relevant degree. This applies to an engineer, professor, barrister, advocate, doctor. Some engineers place their professional title at the end of their names. Doctors and engineers may be addressed using Sahib (Engineer Sahib).

The English and Arabic languages have an influence.

Barbados

Mr Austin L. SEALY

Forms of address in Barbados are the same as for the UK.

Belgium

Mevrouw Veerle DECAVEL

There are three official languages: French, German, and Flemish. To be polite, use the forms of address appropriate to the region concerned.

Whichever language, the family name is the last name in the name string, or the final compound name. Thus: Monsieur Marc DEN DONCKER.

With French, the use of "tu" or "vous" (you) would depend upon the degee of familiarity between the parties, as in France.

Monsieur is placed before appointments and names, but in correspondence do not abbreviate Monsieur to M, nor Madame to Mme, nor Mademoiselle to Mlle., though it is acceptable on envelopes. Do not address letters to *Monsieur le* ... (as they do in France), just write Monsieur (last name).

Titles are still conferred. Some principal titles:

Prince de (Princesse de)
Duc de (Duchesse de)
Marquis de (Marquise de)
Comte de (Comtesse de)
Vicomte de (Vicomtesse de)
Baron de (Baronne de)

Other titles, some of which are hereditary, are: Chevalier, Ritter, Cavaliere, etc.

The envelope should be addressed: "Comte de ..." or "Comtesse de". It is not unusual to add Monsieur or Madame or Mademoiselle before the title.

In German, written and oral forms of address correspond to those used in Germany. Use Herr, Frau, and Fräulein.

In Flemish, which is similar to Dutch but is a dialect that differs in pronunciation:

Mr = *De Heer*   Mrs = *Mevrouw*   Miss = *Mejuffrouw*

The Flemish use of titles is less formal than in Holland.

Persons with conferred or hereditary titles in the German and Flemish speaking parts of Belgium use their own alternatives for the above courtesy titles, but they are too numerous to be listed here in their entirety.

Belize

Mr Marinus Gerardus PLOEG

Forms of address in Belize are the same as for the UK.

Belorus

Spadar Alexander LUKACHENKA

IN BELORUSSIAN:

Mr = *Spadar*   Mrs = *Spadarynya*   Miss = *Spadarynya*

In correspondence abbreviate to:

Spad.   *Sp-Ma.*   *Sp-Ma.*

Address people by their last name, which is the family name. Thus: Spader Lukachenka. Informally you may address someone by their first name. Thus: Alexander.

The patronymic system does not apply.

Benin

Monsieur DOSSOV Paul

Use French honorifics:

Mr = *Monsieur*   Mrs = *Madame*   Miss = *Mademoiselle*

The family name appears *first*, thus: *Dossov Paul* where the family name is *Dossov* and the given name is *Paul*. This applies for both formal and informal use.

When the family name ends in *-gno(e)* or similar, it usually signifies a tribal line of descent, but this is not an important consideration for forms of address.

There are neither hereditary nor conferred titles.

Apply the customary French courtesies when addressing persons of position. Thus: Monsieur l'Ambassadeur, Monsieur le Consul, etc.

However, there are no particular forms of address for those with professional qualifications.

Bhutan

KARMA

The official languages are Dzongkha, Nepali, and English.

This is a matriarchal society, with property passing through the female line, so it is not important to have a family name to pass on down the generations. Many people, especially those in rural areas, have only one name. Consequently, honorifics are not much used.

Amongst the more educated, particularly in and around Thimpu, the capital, there is now a trend towards Westernising name structures. This is taking root slowly and haphazardly. The family procedure is to adopt the village of one's birth as a surname. Thus Karma, who comes from Ura, will be known as *Karma Ura*. "Ura" is not a family name, and it is not passed on to the offspring.

However, the last name of *King Jigme Singye Wangchuck* is a family name in the sense that it is passed on, for he succeeded his father, *Jigme Dorji Wangchuck*. As Royalty was introduced to Bhutan this century (1907), the concept of hereditary family names is relatively modern. The King is addressed as *His Majesty*; this is important and the correct form of address because this distinguishes him from the Indian concept of Maharajahs.

In Dzongkha, the King is known as *Druk Gyalpo* (meaning: the Dragon King), so is referred to and addressed as *His Majesty, Druk Gyalpo*.

Another exception is the *Dorji* family, which is related to the King through marriage; whose name also passes down. This applies to no-one else.

The King's sisters and aunts are addressed as *Royal Highness*, and are bestowed with the title *Ashi*. Thus: *Her Royal Highness Ashi Kesang Wangmo Wangchuck*.

Male members of the Royal family may be made a *Dasho* by the King as an honour or indication of rank. Address them as *Dasho* with all names.

Government Ministers are addressed as *Lyonpo* (with all names).

The majority of people's names are gender-neutral, comparable to

Tibet. The name "Wangchuck" identifies many people in Bhutan, not just the King, but with commoners it can be the first or second name and may be spelt many ways.

Oral and written forms of address are applied in the same way.

Bolivia

Señorita Marta BOSACOMA Bonel

See also the chapter on Spanish American forms of address.

SPANISH IS SPOKEN.

Mr = Señor   Mrs = Señora   Miss = *Señorita*

In correspondence abbreviate to:

Sr.   Sra.   Srta.

The given name is followed by the father's surname, then the mother's surname.

The honorific is followed by the father's surname, thus *Señorita Bosacoma*.

Address correspondence using all names, thus: *Señorita Marta Bosacoma Bonel*.

Married women use *Señora* followed by the given name, father's surname, "de" (of), then their husband's surname. Orally, one would normally address and refer to a married woman by her prefered surname, e.g. *Señora Campora* or *Señora de Campora*. For verbal communication, *Señora Díaz de Campora* is too long. The same applies to unmarried women. *Señorita María García* is too long, so one would tend to say *Señorita García* in conversation. In writing, use the full name.

There are neither hereditary nor conferred titles.

Professional titles

Someone with a degree in engineering is called *Ingeniero* (m)/ *Ingeniera* (f), and someone with a university degree in any subject is a *Licenciado* (m)/or *Licenciada* (f). A medical doctor or person with a doctorate in any discipline is a *Doctor/a*. In oral address use the professional title followed by the father's surname. Thus: Dra. Bosacoma.

When writing, use Ing., Lic., Dr., respectively, but follow the professional title with the given name, the father's surname, then the mother's surname. Thus: *Lic. Marta Bosacoma Bonel*.

When writing, it is optional whether or not to place the honorific before the courtesy title, though the trend now is not to bother. Do not do so when speaking.

Eminent persons are addressed as Señor *Don* for men, and Señora *Doña* for women, followed by the given name, but it is becoming less frequently used and generally one applies it only to formal invitations. In general, address eminent people orally without the honorific, using the Christian name. Thus: *Don Carlos*, and *Doña Marta*.

A Minister is addressed orally as Señor Ministro (Minister). An ambassador is Señor Embajador. When writing, begin with the complete name and rank, followed by the title of office. Thus: Dr. Orlando Morales García, Ministro de Turismo.

Bosnia & Herzegovina

Profesor Zeljko BUJAS (Croatian)
Gospodin Nail KOLIC (Muslim)
Gospodin Radomir JERGIC (Serb)

Use the forename followed by the surname. Thus Antun Cvitan should be addressed as *Gospodin Antun Cvitan*, and (as above) *Profesor Zeljko Bujas*.

For official correspondence, use *only* the surname.

In the vernacular:

Mr = *Gospodin*   Mrs = *Gospodja*   Miss = *Gospodjica*.

Thus: *Gospodjica Ana Cvitan.*

It is the same when writing.

Persons with academic degrees should be addressed accordingly. For instance:

masc.	fem.	
Inziner	Inzinjerka	for a person with a degree in engineering.
Doktor	Doktorica	for a PhD or as a medical qualification.
Magistar	Magistar	before the name of someone with a Master's degree. When writing use "mr" (in small letters).

It is acceptable to address people orally just as Magistar, Profesor, etc, though it is much more congenial to say Magistar Bujas.

Botswana

Miss Mmamosadinyana Punkie Josephine MOLEFE

Forms of address in Botswana are essentially the same as for the UK.

In the expansive example above, the length of Miss MOLEFE's name is not unusual – many people have long names.

In the above name string the tribal name appears first: *Mmamosadinyana*, which usually has a meaning (*queen*, in this example). Then come the baptismal names – there are two in our example but other people might have more or fewer. She will be addressed formally as *Miss Molefe*. Friends call her *Punkie* because that is the forename she has selected as most appropriate.

Tribal chiefs used to be addressed out of respect with a title equivalent to My Lord, but the practice is diminishing and is now largely regarded as unimportant. Chiefs should now be addressed as *Sir* (alone) on first reference, then *Chief*.

Brazil

Senhor FREDERICO César de Araújo

Address people as:

Mr = *Senhor*   Mrs = *Senhora*   Miss = *Senhorita*

However, older unmarried women are addressed as Senhora.

Forms of address correspond largely to those used in Portugal but with some noticeable exceptions.

It is considered politer to address men and women formally by using the honorific with just the first name. Thus: Senhor Frederico. The other names are not used, however long the name string.

When informality is appropriate just use the first name without the honorific.

In the name string men often place their mother's maiden name before the father's surname.

A married lady may retain her maiden surname before her married surname, and her father's surname as well.

It is not customary to use the *de* in someone's name when speaking to them, nor is it used in correspondence unless the recipient has explicitly incorporated it into their name to suggest it is required.

When writing, the use of all names is not compulsory; use the honorific with the first and final names (with appropriate pronoun). Thus: Senhor Brenho (de Souza Brasil Dias) Da Costa.

"*Dom*" is used when addressing priests.
"*Dona*" is placed after Senhora when writing formally to a lady. It is also used in speech to acquaintances. Thus: *Dona Maria* . . .

Professional titles

Address a professor as such. In writing, Prof. is used as an abbreviation only for ordinary schoolmasters. It is no longer necessary to say Senhor Professor.

Address a doctor as Doutor, an engineer as Engenheiro, an architect as Arquitecto.

Those with degrees in law, with a Licenciado (Master), or Bacharel (Bachelor), are all styled Doutor (abbreviate to *Dr.* in correspondence). "Doutor" is therefore applied to everyone with a degree except for those specified above.

Courtesy titles:

Use Ilustríssimo and Ilustríssima (often abbreviated to Ilmo. and Ilma. in correspondence) to address senior people in business, such as the president of a company. Thus: Ilustríssimo Senhor César.

Similarly, use Excellentíssimo and Excelentíssima to address, for instance, persons with high political office, such as ambassadors, again inserting the usual honorific, thus: Excellentíssimo Senhor César. Alternatively, a Minister is addressed orally as Senhor Ministro/Senhora Ministra, an Ambassador is Senhor Ambaixador / Senhora Embaixadora.

In correspondence, write Sua Excêlencia, followed by rank.

> His/Her Excellency = Sua Excêlencia
> Distinguished gentleman = Exmo Sr.
> Your Excellency = Excêlencia

Brunei

Awang ALI Fadzil bin Haji Sapar

There are no family names for Muslims. Address people by their *first name*, Thus: Mr JAINI Abdullah.

One may address ordinary citizens as Mr, Mrs, Miss. In the vernacular, this is *Awang* (Mr), and *Dayang* (Mrs/Miss), but sometimes men prefer to be addressed as "Master" instead.

A woman retains her maiden name upon marriage. She should always be addressed as "Dayang".

There are several alternatives available when addressing men. I have already mentioned that some men prefer to be called *Master*. There are many men who are distinguished from other ordinary citizens by having the honorific "*Awangku*" as long as they remain single. This signifies a historic relationship to the royal family. Upon marriage, an *Awangku* becomes a "*Pengiran*". It is therefore a hereditary title. Do NOT address them as Mr (*Awang*).

Note that an *Awang* who marries remains an *Awang*.

Sometimes, usually in formal situations, *bin* (son of) is applied, Arab-style, as with the example at the head of this chapter. Similarly, a female would use *binti* (daughter of). *Haji* is used by men and *Hajah* by women to signify the person has visited Mecca. If one's father has been to Mecca, *Haji* (abbreviated to *Hj*) will follow *bin* or *binti*, as with: *Hj Morshidi bin Hj Mohamad Yussof* (who will addressed as *Awang Haji MORSHIDI*). The styles described in this paragraph should be included for highly formal correspondence but may be disregarded for oral purposes. For informal correspondence he may be addressed as *Awang Haji Morshdi Yussof.*

Here is an example of the name string of a person entitled to be addressed as *Pengiran*:

Honorfic	Indicates he has been to Mecca	Given name	Father's title	Father has been to Mecca	Family name
Pengiran	Haji	Omar	Pengiran	Haji	Ali

He should be addressed formally in speech as Pengiran Haji Omar Ali, less formally as Pengiran Omar.

In formal correspondence address him with the full name string, or, in informal correspondence, as Pg. Omar Ali.

Pengiran Omar's wife will also be addressed as *Pengiran*.

Other titles, that are bestowed by the Sultan:

Dato (m) / Datin (f) – highest award.
Pehin (m) – next highest award.

Some people have both awards and are addressed as *Pehin Dato* . . .

The correct oral form of address for the Sultan, and for his wife, the Sultana, is *Your Highness*. When writing, address correspondence to His (or Her) Highness (or Their Highnesses). It may be abbreviated, so H. H. Sultan Bolkiah.

The Chinese community are similarly addressed by their *first name*, though this time the first name is also the family name. Thus: *Mr HOE Siang Teo*. When familiarity is appropriate use just the two given names in union as if they are one: *Siang Teo*. This custom applies to men and women alike.

Bulgaria

Gospodin Zahari Mitev RADOUKOV

Mr = *Gospodin*, Mrs = *Gospozha*, Miss = *Gospojitsa*

(Note that Russia does not use Gospojitsa).

Bulgarian names are constructed with a patronymic pattern resembling that of Russia.

The forename (or first name) is followed by the patronymic, which shows filiation to the father – then comes the family name, which is passed on down the generations. Zahari Mitev Radoukov would be addressed as Zahari Radoukov. Thus: *Gospodin Radoukov*.

Zahari Radoukov might have a son with the given name Ivan. He will be known as Ivan Zahariev Radoukov.

So always address people by the honorific with their last name (family name) unless there is familiarity, when you use their first name alone. Never use the middle name as a form of address. It is used mainly for the telephone directory and official papers (though not necessarily).

A name change upon marriage is optional; some women do not accept their husband's family name. Those women that change their names adopt their husband's surname but feminise the ending. Thus *Mr Petrov, Mrs Petrova*. Another example: *Mr Dobrovski, Mrs Dobrovska*. The femine ending for *-ski* is *-ska*.

If talking about someone you can use the surname as a means of identification.

When addressing persons of rank or with a professional qualification, you should use only the family name. Thus: *Zahari Mitev Radoukov* would be addressed as *Professor Radoukov*. Professional degrees are not widely used, but when applied say Architect / Engineer / Advocate (then family name).

Burkina Faso

Monsieur Salifou Rigobert KONGO

French is used exclusively for official and commercial purposes. Use the usual French forms of address.

Mr = *Monsieur*,   Mrs = *Madame*,   Miss = *Mademoiselle*

Burma (Myanmar)

U HTAY Aung

There is no comparable system to that of the customary Mr, Mrs, and Miss. Instead, you face a labyrinth of curious forms of address that will test your powers of observation.

Men	Orally	In Writing
A male under 30 (including children, should be addressed as: It is also used sometimes to show humility.	Maung	Mg
A male aged 30–45 should be addressed: Literal meaning: elder brother.	Ko	Ko
Example: Aung Gyi, in his thirties, will be addressed as *Ko Aung Gyi*.		
(Note: Maung is also a common name, often repeated. Therefore avoid confusion by addressing a man under 30 whose *name* is Maung Maung as *Ko Maung Maung*).		
A male aged 45+ should be addressed: (pronounced "OO") Literal meaning: Uncle.	U	U
Military officers and sometimes personalities regarded as leaders	Bo	Bo

Women	Orally	In Writing
A female under 35 (including children) should be addressed as: Note: In practice, one can use Ma for any woman up to about 50 years old because Ma carries no particular status.	Ma	Ma

A woman older than 35, especially if older than 50, should be addressed:	Daw	Daw
Any woman, regardless of age, who has "status' or qualifications, such as teachers, lawyers, etc. should be addressed:	Daw	Daw
There is no distinction in terms of forms of address between married and single women, so address them as Ma or Daw.		

Thakin, placed before the first name, meaning master, was introduced by nationalist politicians during colonial days to persuade the British colonialists to address them on equal terms. It was a gender-neutral form of address that rose to prominence during the 1930s, and faded away after 1948. Elderly Burmese remember it with nostalgic affection.

A person is traditionally named according to the day of birth, each day having several names to choose from – for example, Kyaw or Kyi if born on a Monday. Local names could be confusing to foreigners since they can be duplicated in many variations; moreover, the phonetic pronunciation is not completely the same as the Roman alphabet.

The family name, in the loosest sense, is the first name in the string. With friends, use *Ma* if they are younger than you, whether male or female. Otherwise use *Ko* (for males, as per above table). Close friends will use the first name (family name) only. Business acquaintances should always use both names. Thus: (for males) *U Chit Hla*.

Do NOT use *Mr* with *U*, because Mr *is* U.

Women do not change their names upon marriage. Both men and women retain their names throughout. Children do not take their parent's name.

When corresponding, for instance, to (in Western idiom) Mr & Mrs

Aung Bwa, persons of status whose acquaintance you have made, it is acceptable to address them (both) as *U Aung Bwa*, where the use of U shows respect. However, if they are strangers and have no particular status, address them separately. Thus: Ko Aung Bwa and Daw May May Khin.

If they are married but less than 30 years old, he would be addressed as U, and she as Ma. Thus: U Chit Hla and Ma Ye Htut.

There are further complications in terms of family lineage. For instance, the eldest son takes his father's first (family) name. Thus: U Chit Hla's eldest son would be Ko Chit Aye.

The eldest daughter takes her mother's first (family) name, then her father's.

Families also tend to make up the rules as they go along, so I shall expand no further.

Thankfully, there are no conferred or hereditary titles.

Burundi

Monsieur Canut NIYONKURU

The national language is Kirundi, but French is widely used and is also the administrative language.

Mr = *Monsieur*   Mrs = *Madame*   Miss = *Mademoiselle*

Cambodia

Mith MAO Mayan

There are many traps for the unwary in the correct use of honorifics. They are important social pointers because they indicate degrees of respect and rank.

Use the first name alone unless you are addressing a person of a higher status or of the same status as yourself. Thus, ordinary citizen Mao Mayan should be *Mr Mao*, and Sok Chuor should be *Mr Sok*.

Use "Mith" when addressing friends. Thus: *Mith Mao*.

For ordinary women use "Oum Bong" or "Bong Srey". For ordinary men use "Oum Bong". It is impolite to omit "Bong".

These honorifics mean "you". But it is rude to address a person of status as "you".

Nor may a monk be addressed as "You". Instead, say "*Prek Som*".

Minister Hun Sen may be addressed by foreigners as *Mr Sen*, but it is politer to address him as *Ta* Hun Sen, saying both names, as "Ta" acknowledges his elevated status.

"Ek Oukdom" replaces "Ta" when addressing Members of Parliament, though in informal surroundings family and close friends will use "Ta".

"Lok Srey" precedes the name of a woman of rank in government. Someone addressed as "Lok" Chung Tiew would be a high ranking man, or could also be the husband of an Ek Oukdom.

King Norodom Sihanouk is known as "Somdak" (King), as are his sons, though they are princes. Use the last name first after the title.

King Sihanouk would be properly addressed as *Somdak Prek Sihanouk.*

Here is a menu of titles granted by the King, His Majesty Preah Bat Samdech Preah Norodom Sihanouk Varman, to members of the inner Royal Family:

- Samdech Krom Preah – currently HRH Prince Norodom Ranariddh. Samdech is a title of nobility and by rank they are first.
- Sdech Krom Luong – currently HRH Prince Norodom. A Sdech is not as high as a Samdech, but is higher than that of a simple Royal Highness. There is no distinction between a civilian Samdech and one who is a member of the Royal Family. Their order of precedence is dictated by their state functions and by the seniority of their nomination as Samdech.
- Sdech Krom Khun – currently HRHs Princes Norodom Chakrapong, Norodom Sihammoni, and Norodom Sirivudh.

These titles indicate the rank of the senior Princes, but should not be taken as an indication as to which will become King.

Other Titles

- Samdech Chakrey – normally granted to the most senior military chiefs or the Minister of Defence.
- Samdech Preah Reach Kanitha – normally granted to the King's proper sister or to a cousin elevated to the rank of Samdech "younger sister" of the King.
- Samdech Reach Botrei Preah Ream – normally granted to the King's eldest daughter.
- The Royal Princess – a daughter of the King, who is ranked immediately after the Sdechs but before the other Royal Highnesses.

Note that titles of nobility defer to the titles held by State authorities by way of protocol. Thus a Prime Minister is more important than a Samdech.

Cameroun

Madame Cecile Asseng NGUELE

Bilingual in French and English, though most people are inclined to use French forms of address in East Cameroun.

Mr = *Monsieur*   Mrs = *Madame*   Miss = Mademoiselle

As stated, French is used for business and in official circles in East Cameroun, but most people in West Cameroun speak and use English forms of address, though spoken English would be Pidgin.

Canada

Mr David ATKINSON

In the English-speaking provinces forms of address are very much the same as for the UK. There are some differences, however:

Women generally do not take their husband's name upon marriage; they retain their maiden name. This applies especially to the younger generation, though this practice is widespread. Each province imposes its own legal formula, and we understand that most of them prescribe that a woman legally keeps her maiden name upon marriage. Some women will use their maiden name in formal situations and for business whilst using their married name for social purposes. Those that do so often hyphenate their maiden and married names. The family's children have the option of taking the father's family name, or the mother's, or to hyphenate them. About 40% of children adopt their father's family name, and the other 60% are divided between taking the mother's and taking both.

When corresponding with Members of Parliament the initials MLA (Member of the Legislative Assembly) should be placed after the name. Thus, *Mr Eaton MLA*.

Ministers are addressed orally and in correspondence as *The Honourable*.

There is a Federal honours system, but it imposes no change to the way people are addressed save that the initials of the honour follow the name.

Quebec

In Quebec, forms of address are in French and correspond largely to French custom.

Use:

Mr = *Monsieur*   Mrs = *Madame*   Miss = *Mademoiselle*

Please see the chapter on France.

In correspondence there is a difference to the French style in that you should address someone (as in the UK) by their first name followed by their family name. In France it is the other way around.

There are no titles.

Women do not take their husband's name upon marriage; this is enshrined in provincial legislation. The family's children have the option of taking the father's family name, or the mother's, or of hyphenating them.

Cape Verde

Senhor Fernando Jorge Wahnon FERREIRA

Portuguese is the official language but Crioulo (a mixture of Portuguese and West African dialects) is the lingua franca. Portuguese speakers apparently have difficulty communicating in some of the 10 islands that comprise Cape Verde, but you are advised to use Portuguese forms of address nevertheless. Please refer to the chapter on Portugal.

When addressing people orally:

Mr = *Senhor*   Mrs / Miss = *Senhora*

Unmarried women are also addressed as *Minha Senhora*.

Use the honorific with the last name only.

In correspondence open with Dear Sir / Dear Madam by using *Exmo* (m) or *Exma* (f). Thus: Exmo Senhor, and Exma Senhora.

Men usually include their mother's maiden name before their father's surname. A married woman may retain her maiden surname before her married surname.

It is customary to address people with professional qualifications by placing the title after the honorific, as with: *Senhor Doutor* (doctor – do not abbreviate) and *Senhor Engenheiro* (an engineer).

Cayman Islands

John EBANKS

Forms of address correspond to those used in the UK.

As an informal local custom, some people address one another with the honorific and first name. Thus: *Mr John*. Foreign visitors are not expected to do this.

There are many merchant seamen, though mostly retired, who are in the habit of being addressed as *Captain* (then family name).

Central African Republic

Monsieur Germain GRESENGUET

The national language is Sanjho, but French is the administrative language and is widely used.

Mr = Monsieur   *Mrs = Madame*   *Miss = Mademoiselle*

Chad

Madame Aziza Baroud ISMAEL

French is widely spoken and is the first official language. The second is Arabic, though a local dialect is used.

WHEN USING FRENCH:

Mr = *Monsieur*   Mrs = *Madame*   Miss = *Mademoiselle*

and forms of address correspond largely to those used in France.

WHEN USING ARABIC:

Mr = *Asayid*   Mrs / Miss = *Asayeda*

When writing to someone in Arabic it is sometimes customary to insert the preposition *al* (of) before the family name. Thus : Idris Adjidé would be addressed as *Idris al-Adjidé*.
The preposition is not used in speech.

Chile

Señor Juan Eduardo EGUIGUREN Ibanee

See also the chapter on Spanish American forms of address.

SPANISH IS SPOKEN.

Mr = *Señor*   Mrs = *Señora*   Miss = *Señorita*

In correspondence abbreviate to:

Sr.   Sra.   Sta.

The given name is followed by the father's surname, then the mother's surname. Thus: Señor Juan Eduardo EGUIGUREN Ibanee. Target the father's surname and say: Señor *Eguiguren*.

Sometimes two Christian names precede the family name. They may have to be said together, without separation. Knowing when is really a matter of experience and a question of tone. With friends, it is usual to use only the first name. Otherwise, use either.

Señorita is always used for an unmarried lady regardless of her age.

Married women use Señora followed by the given name, father's surname, "de" (of), then their husband's surname. In writing, use the name in full. However, some people drop the "de" in correspondence, though it is not incorrect to keep it. Orally, one would normally address and refer to a married woman by her prefered surname, e.g. *Señora Campora* or *Señora de Campora*. For verbal communication, *Señora Díaz de Campora* is too long. The same applies to unmarried women. *Srta. María García* is too long, so one would tend to say *Srta. García* in conversation.

Children will take both the father's and mother's surnames.

When writing, use all names, whether to men or women.

If you are looking up the telephone directory, names appear in this order: Father's surname / mother's surname / given names. Thus: *Eguiguren Ibanee, Juan Eduardo.*

There are neither hereditary nor conferred titles.

In correspondence it is usual to sign off with Atentamente (Yours sincerely).

When writing to persons of distinction it is customary to open with the title, for instance: *Señor Ministro* (Minister). Similarly, an Ambassador should be addressed as *Su Excelencia* (Your Excellency) – followed by forename(s) and family name.

There are no special forms of address for persons with professional qualifications except for doctors of medicine (*Dr. Julio Pérez Soto*) and professors. When addressing a doctor or professor, place the titles between Señor and the name. Thus: *Señor Dr. Eguiguren.*

Note that the honorifics Don and Doña are seldom used.

China

Mr WANG Xiaoyuan

The family name precedes the given name. Thus: Mr Wang Xiaoyuan is *Mr Wang*, and Zhu Zushou should be addressed as *Mr Zhu*.

Similarly, Gu Jingxian would be *Madame Gu* or *Mrs Gu*. Many married women prefer to be addressed as Madame. Women do not change their name upon marriage.

If you are addressing people in Chinese:

> Mr = *Xiansheng* (thus: Wang Xiansheng)   Mrs = *Taitai*
> (thus Gu Taitai)   Ms = *Xiaoniang* (thus: Gu Xiaoniang)

Friends use the given name only. Thus: *Xiaoyuan, Zushou,* and *Jingxian* respectively.

There are neither hereditary nor conferred titles.

Chinese tend to prefer formality, especially between persons of unequal status (teacher / student; employer / employee, etc). Those thus elevated should be addressed as Mr/Mrs/Miss, and they will address those beneath them without the honorific, using the given name only.

There are professional titles. Using someone with the name Wu Taozhang as our example, a student would say *Teacher Wu* (Wu Laoshi). But if you are addressing the teacher in English, the usual honorific may be preferred. Engineers, and others with professions, will probably expect to be addressed as such. Use their business cards for a clue. Between businessmen, *Mr Wu* is the safest bet.

China's move towards capitalism has generated a new breed of young entrepreneurs who tend to prefer less formality than older management in state enterprises. The use of *Comrade* (Tongzhi) has probably all but died out, but obsequious waiters and fawning taxi drivers may call potential big-tippers *Master* (Shifu). There is also some official resistance to change. The organisation department of the Communist Party in Shanghai has issued a command for all party members to use *Tongzhi* instead of titles, though so far this edict is confined to party members in Shanghai.

Many Chinese adopt their childhood nicknames and retain them throughout life. This often leads to fairly bizarre situations. The prefix *Xiao* in *Wu Xiaozhang* can mean *small* and may have been used by others as a diminutive when Mr Wu was a child. In the countryside particularly, people may often address each other, for instance, as Fatty Wu, or Spotty Ma, even though they may no longer be fat or spotty. In an urban and business context, this is probably less likely.

Tibet

Tibetan society in general does not use honorifics, and Tibetan names are similarly innocent of gender and of the Western concept of a family name or surname.

Therefore *Tserring Tashi* might be male or female. For our purposes he is male. When addressing him, even in formal circumstances, use just the names; do not use *Mr*. The names are inter-changeable, so might appear in any order, and you may use either or any.

The suffix *La* is used as a term of familiarity when addressing an elder or senior, usually with those in government service and between close friends. Thus: *Tserring Tashi La*.

The principle exception to omitting the honorific is when addressing senior religious figures. Address such a person as *Geyshe* (father), using the word either on its own or followed by his names.

Footnote

The pronunciation of Chinese names for non-Chinese speakers is tricky at best, and differences in dialects and the romanisation systems do little to help.

For example, China's former paramount leader found his name written sometimes as Deng Xiaoping, and at other times as Teng Hsiao-P'ing. In any case, remember that the second and third syllables are always pronounced as one word, whether they are written separately, hyphenated, or as one word.

There are at least 55 minority groups in China with languages such as Hakka, Miao, Yi, etc. as well as many localised regional dialects of Chinese, such as Cantonese, Shanghainese, Hokien (in Fujian) etc. However, nearly everyone speaks Mandarin, the national language and the language of the Han Chinese, the ethnic majority.

In Singapore, for instance, many people speak Hokien (though most will also speak Mandarin); in Taiwan they speak Mandarin, but in Hong Kong they speak mostly Cantonese.

However, the meaning of Chinese characters will be the same to everyone though their pronunciation may be different. This applies to names too.

A Chinese name is usually made up of three characters, each expressing a different meaning. Name choice is a delicate art settled at birth, frequently by comparing the characters to the five elements to achieve a name with harmony and equilibrium.

When we distinguish given names, for example, by using a hyphen in the Taiwan chapter, separating them into monosyllables in the Singapore chapter, or compounding them in the China chapter, we are applying the transliteration system commonly used in those countries. So the name Ma Zhushi (Pinyin transliteration method) may be written as Ma Zhu-shih (Wade-Giles method), though pronunciation is the same.

Colombia

Señor Luis PRIETO-Ocampo

See also the general chapter on Spanish American forms of address.

SPANISH IS SPOKEN.

Mr = *Señor*   Mrs = *Señora*   Miss = *Señorita*

In correspondence abbreviate to:

Sr.   Sra.   Srta.

The given name is followed by the father's surname, then the mother's surname.

Address a man by his father's surname. Thus: Señor *Prieto*.

Address a married woman as Señora followed by her maiden name, or her husband's family name, divided by "de" (of). Thus: *Señora de Prieto*.

A married woman may decide to keep her maiden names instead of using her husband's family name. Otherwise she will use her first name followed by her maiden name then her husband's family name. Thus: Luz (first name) Marina (maiden name) de Prieto (husband's family name).

A young unmarried woman would be addressed as Señorita. A more mature woman would be addressed as Señora whether married or not.

There are no hereditary titles.

The courtesy titles *Don* and *Doña* are sometimes used in writing for eminent persons: Señor Don (m) or *Señora Doña* (f) followed by the given name. Thus: *Señor* Don Luis.

Professional people should be addressed orally and in correspondence as Doctor (m) / Doctora (f). Note how this applies to everyone with a degree except for the exceptions given below. In each case follow with the family name, as identified above. *Licenciado* is not used.

A doctor of medicine is also a doctor, without distinction.

Do not precede these titles with the honorific (saying or writing *Señor Doctor* . . . is wrong).

	Abbrev. for correspondence	Masc.	Fem.
Doctor	Dr./Dra.	Doctor	Doctora
Ingeniero (engineer)	Ing.	Señor Ingeniero	Señora Ingeniera
Profesor	Prof.	Señor Profesor	Señora Profesora
Arquitecto (architect)	Arquitecto	Señor Arquitecto	Señora Arquitecta

Address an ambassador orally as Señor Embajador / Señora Embajadora. In correspondence use Su Excelencia Doctor(a) . . .

For a minister say Señor Ministro (Señora Ministra).

Comoros

Said ALI Muhammad Allaoui
(or: Monsieur ALI)

French is for official use, but the national language is a dialect of Swahili.

Comoros was first settled by Arabs about 1,000 years ago. Arab forms of address apply (see general chapter on Arab forms), but the usual French forms of address are acceptable. Use:

Mr = *Monsieur*   Mrs = *Madame*   Miss = *Mademoiselle*

Congo

Monsieur Jean-Marie EWENGUE

FRENCH IS SPOKEN.

Mr = *Monsieur*   Mrs = *Madame*   Miss = *Mademoiselle*

Costa Rica

Señora Alba DOMÍNGUEZ de Farhat

See also the chapter on Spanish American forms of address.

SPANISH IS SPOKEN.

Mr = *Señor*   Mrs = *Señora*   Miss = *Señorita*

In correspondence abbreviate to:

Sr.   Sra.   Srta.

The given name is followed by the father's surname, then the mother's surname.

Address a man by his father's family name. Thus: *Señor Domínguez.*

In writing, married women use Señora followed by the given name, father's surname, then "de" (of), then husband's surname. Orally, one would normally address and refer to a married woman by her prefered surname, e.g. *Señora Campora* or *Señora de Campora*. For verbal communication, *Señora Díaz de Campora* is too long. The same applies to unmarried women. *Srta. María García* is too long, so one would tend to say *Srta. García* in conversation.

If writing to the husband and wife together, when the wife is not using her husband's family name address them like this: *Señor Carlos Domínguez Vargas* and *Señora María García Garde*.

A young unmarried woman would be addressed as Señorita. A more mature woman would be addressed as Señora whether married or not.

The courtesy titles *Don* and *Doña* are used for eminent and older persons. Say: *Don* (m) or *Doña* (f) followed by the given name (first name). Thus: *Don Luis*. It is not necessary to use the honorific with the courtesy title.

There are no hereditary or conferred titles.

Professional titles

Someone with a degree in engineering is called Ingeniero (m) or Ingeniera (f), and someone with a university degree in any subject at post graduate level is a Licenciado (m) or Licenciada (f). A medical doctor or person with a doctorate in any discipline is a Doctor (m) or Doctora (f). In oral address use the professional title followed by the father's surname. Thus: *Dr. Domínguez*.

Note that Grammar School teachers are addressed as Maestro (m) or Maestra (f), and High School teachers are addressed as Profesor (m) or Profesora (f).

In correspondence use Ing., Lic., Dr., (as appropriate) but begin with the professional title followed by the given name, father's surname, then the mother's surname. Thus: *Dr. Orlando Morales García*. It is not necessary to use the honorific as well.

A Minister is addressed orally as *Señor Ministro* (Minister). An ambassador is *Señor Embajador*. When writing, begin with the complete name and rank. Thus: *Dr. Orlando Morales García, Ministro de Turismo*.

Côte d'Ivoire (Ivory Coast)

Monsieur Ervais Assui DELON

French is used exclusively for official and commercial purposes.

Mr = *Monsieur*   Mrs = *Madame*   Miss = *Mademoiselle*

When addressing correspondence place the family name first, then the given name(s). In conversation it is the other way around. Therefore address your letter to *Monsieur Delon, Ervais Assui* – open with *Dear Monsieur Delon* – and speak of *Ervais Assui Delon*.

Refer to chapter on France.

Croatia

Gospodin Antun CVITAN

In the vernacular:

Mr = *Gospodin*   Mrs = *Gospodja*   Miss = *Gospodjica*.

Use the forename followed by the surname. Thus *Antun Cvitan* should be addressed as *Gospodin Cvitan*.

Thus: *Gospodjica Ana Cvitan.*

It is the same when writing.

One rarely distinguishes persons with hereditary titles from commoners, but there are signs that titles are slowly returning to fashion. When addressing such personalities precede the above honorifics with *Plemeniti*, *Plemenita*, and *Pleminita* respectively. Thus: *Plemenita Gospodjica Ana Cvitan.*

Persons with academic degrees should be addressed accordingly. For instance:

masc.	Fem.	
Inzenjer	Inzenjerka	for a person with a degree in engineering.
Doktor	Doktorica	for a PhD or as a medical qualification.
Magistar	Magistrica	before the name of someone with a Master's degree. When writing use "mr" (in small letters).

It is acceptable to address people orally just as Magistar, Profesor, etc, though it is much more congenial to say *Magistar Cvitan.*

Cuba

Señor José Manuel ALVAREZ Conesa

See the chapter on Spanish American forms of address.

SPANISH IS SPOKEN.

Mr = *Señor*   Mrs = *Señora*   Miss = *Señorita*

In correspondence abbreviate to:

Sr.   *Sra.*   *Srta.*

The given name(s) is followed by the father's surname, then the mother's surname. The Father's surname is the one commonly used. Thus: *Señor Alvarez*.

Say the honorific followed by the father's surname, but when writing use all names.

In writing, married women use Señora followed by the given name, and father's surname (they do not add their husband's surname). In oral address, as in English, use the honorific plus surname (Señora/Señorita Alvarez).

There are neither hereditary nor conferred titles.

Professional titles

Someone with a degree in engineering is called Ingeniero (m) or Ingeniera (f), and someone with a university degree in any subject is a Licenciado (m) or Licenciada (f). Abbreviate in correspondence to Ing. and Lic. respectively.

People with a degree in any discipline, as well as medical doctors, are also addressed as *doctor/a*. In oral address use the professional title followed by the father's surname. Thus: Dr. Bosacoma.

Note that Grammar School teachers are addressed as Maestro (m) or Maestra (f), and High School teachers are addressed as Profesor (m) or Profesora (f).

When writing, use the full name string.

Do not use the honorific with the courtesy title. Thus *Señor Dr.* is wrong.

Don (m) and Doña (f) are used as a form of respect when addressing older people (as distinct from eminent people). They are applied instead of Señor or Señora but are followed by the given name (Don José).

A Minister is addressed orally as *Señor Ministro* (Minister). An ambassador is *Señor Embajador*. When writing, begin with the complete name and rank, followed by the title of office. Thus: *Dr. Orlando Morales García, Ministro de Turismo.*

American and English words are creeping into modern Cuban language but have yet to affect forms of address.

Cyprus

Mr Angelos M. ANGELIDES

Forms of address follow U.K. custom, with family names appearing last, for speech and social correspondence. Note that all nouns are declinable.

For official correspondence, such as in government departments, banks, large organisations, etc, place the family name first, then the given name. Note that Angelos Angelides would therefore become Angelides Angelos.

Mr = *Kyrios*   Mrs = *Kyria*   Miss = *Despoinida*.

Abbreviate Kyrios to k. (small k) in correspondence. Thus: k. Volioti (An alternative abbreviation is, as it most often appears, kon; as this form declines, it is best avoided by non-Greek speakers).
Similarly, abbreviate Kyria to Ka, as with Ka Volioti.
Abbreviate Despoinida to Dis. Thus: Dis Volioti.

There is no equivalent to the use of Ms.

As a general rule of translation, transliteration of Greek words is only used in English where a translation does not exist. Where there is an equivalent word in English (as *Mr* for *k.*), the English form is preferable (so: "Mr Angelos Angelides", or "A. Angelides). Also in some instances where there is an English equivalent for certain first names, like Constantine for Constantinos, George for Giorgos, John for Yiannis, etc., use of the English name is quite acceptable and often preferable.

Women tend to adopt their husband's family name upon marriage, but not always. There is now an inclination to hyphenate the maiden name to the husband's.

It is usual for a person's name to include their father's initial in the middle. Thus: *Angelos M. Angelides*.

We are advised that poorly educated people tend to say, for example, *Mrs firstname*, but it is incorrect. One should properly use the honorific before the family name.

There are no titles of nobility.

Under the Cyprus Constitution no hereditary or conferred titles are permitted.

There are no special forms of address for persons with degrees other than for doctors of medicine and, optionally, for those with PhDs. In correspondence doctors of medicine are also plain *Mr*.

Ministers are addressed as *Kyrie Epourge*. Similarly, Ambassadors are *Kyrie Presvi*.

Cyprus (Turkish Republic of Northern)

Sayın ALI OSMAN

It is wrong to use the forms of address that apply to the Greek portion of Cyprus (as in the previous chapter). Instead, use exactly the same forms of address that are used for Turkey.

The family name is last, but see below.

In semi-formal conversation, and if you are meeting someone for business for the first time, you use the first name followed by *Bey* (for men), or *Bayan* (for women). Thus: Ali Osman would be addressed as *Ali Bey* (without the family name).

In correspondence the order is reversed. Thus: *Bay Ali Osman*, or *Bayan Aliye Osman* (where Bey becomes Bay).

You may also use *Sayın* (meaning Esquire) for both sexes in oral address or correspondence. Thus: *Sayın Ali Osman* (both names).

However, for formal correspondence use *Sayın* followed by the family name. Thus: *Sayın Osman*. Or: *Sayın A. Osman*. If one is to be strictly correct one should use both names, but this is usually too formal for general business purposes. Thus: *Sayın Ali Osman*.

The use of Sayın with Bay (or Bayan) adds prestige and esteem. Thus: *Sayın Bayan Aliye Osman*. There is no distinction between Miss and Mrs.

Women usually adopt their husband's family name upon marriage. However, there is now a trend whereby the woman not only retains her maiden name, but her husband takes her family name.

There are no hereditary or conferred titles.

"Efendi" is used for someone of lower status than the introducer or addresser. Thus "This is Ali Efendi". Use their first name only, with *Efendi* following. The equivalent for a woman is "Hanim".

Czech Republic

Pan Jiří DĚVEČKA

Mr = *Pan*   Mrs = *Paní*   Miss = *Slečna*
(abbreviate Slečna to Sl. in correspondence)

The family name appears last in the name string. Thus Vladimír Děvečka is addressed as *Pan Děvečka*, as with most Western countries.

The majority of women (we understand this applies to about 70%) suffix *-ova* to their family name as a feminine ending, so Mr Děvečka's wife would be *Paní Děvečková*.

The Slovak and Czech Republics employ the same techniques.

The patronymic system does not apply.

Denmark

Herr Hans Christian TEISEN

Mr = *herr*   Mrs = *fru*   Miss = *froken*

In correspondence abbreviate to

hr   fru   fruk.

The Danes consider the use of honorifics to be rather old fashioned and informality is generally preferred. We recommend using them on first introduction only or when the situation is formal.

There is no oral equivalent to Ms, but the abbreviation fr. can be used in correspondence to mean either fru or froken.

A wife usually acquires her husband's name on marriage, but it is becoming widespread for women to retain their maiden name. Hyphenated names (maiden name plus married name) are also fairly common now.

Titles are not usually used on informal occasions.

There are no special forms of address for persons with degrees other than doctors of medicine and those with PhDs. Even so, the honorifics "doktor" and "professor" are only occasionally used. It is acceptable to place the honorific beforehand, as with *herr doktor*, but it is optional.

Ministers, Officers, and Ambassadors may be addressed as minister, kommandør, and ambassadør, though an Ambassador may also be addressed using the Danish form for His Excellency: *deres Excellence*.

Faroe Islands

Note: Danish is spoken in the Faroe Islands, but Faroese forms of address are used:

Mr = harra   Mrs = frû   Miss = frøken
(*frøken* is abbreviated to *frk* in correspondence)

Greenland

There are no honorifics in Greenland, and the custom is to be informal. Just use people's names. Danish and English forms of address may be used if you wish, but it is not necessary to do so.

Djibouti

Monsieur YOUSSOUF OMAR DOUALEH

FRENCH IS SPOKEN.

Mr = *Monsieur*   Mrs = *Madame*   Miss = *Mademoiselle*

Djibouti does not distinguish between forenames and surnames. You are expected to use all names, whether corresponding or speaking. Therefore do not abbreviate when speaking, but take a breath and say them all.

When a woman marries she retains all of her maiden names and tags on all of her husband's names. Being formal, you will be expected to say (or write) them all. Being practical, you may ask her which one to use, when social familiarity is appropriate.

Dominica (Commonwealth of)

Mr Steven Joseph LAROCQUE

Although there is French influence, and the local language is a Creole patois, the official language is English, and the usual UK forms of address apply.

When using Creole forms of address (which are not used for correspondence) say:

Mr = *Messieurs*   Mrs = *Madame*   Miss = *Mademoiselle*
(*Mademoiselle* is often shortened to *Mamselle*)

74

Note that Creole honorifics may be used before either the given name or the surname, though they are more commonly used before the given name.

Dominican Republic

Señor Emilio CASTILLO Delgado

Spanish is spoken.

Mr = *Señor*   Mrs = *Señora*   Miss = *Señorita*

In correspondence abbreviate to:

Sr.   *Sra.*   *Srta.*

The given name is followed by the father's surname, then the mother's surname. The father's surname is the one commonly used.

The honorific is followed by the father's surname. Thus: *Señor Castillo*.
When writing, use all names,

In writing, married women use Señora followed by the given name, father's surname, "de" (of), then husband's surname. Orally, one would normally address and refer to a married woman by her prefered surname, e.g. *Señora Campora* or *Señora de Campora*. For verbal communication, *Señora Díaz de Campora* is too long. The same applies to unmarried women. *Srta. María García* is too long, so one would tend to say *Srta. García* in conversation.

There are neither hereditary nor conferred titles.

Professional titles

Someone with a degree in engineering is called *Ingeniero* (m) or *Ingeniera* (f), and someone with a university degree in any subject is a *Licenciado* (m) or *Licenciada* (f). Abbreviate in correspondence to *Ing.* and *Lic.* respectively.

A medical doctor or person with a doctorate in any discipline is a *doctor/a*. In oral address use the professional title followed by the father's surname.

Don (m) and *Doña* (f) are used as courtesy titles to show respect, though nowadays younger people use them less. Thus: Don Carlos (first name only).

It is optional whether or not to precede the courtesy title with the honorific, as with: Señor Doctor, but in practice do so only in correspondence.

When writing, use the full name string.

Dubai

Sayid ABDULRAHIM Ahmed Mohamad AL-MARRI

Mr = *Sayid*   Mrs = *Sayeda*   Miss = *Anissa*

There are no hard and fast rules with Arab names. Everything is loose and variable, and different influences will govern the practices of each Arab country.

Within the string of Arab names everyone usually has their own given name followed by their father's given name. Thus: *Mohamad Jemal* or *Mohamad bin Jemal*. Complications arise as the string is added to by the practice of honouring ancestors.

Women also derive their names from their father, and sometimes add their father's father, and so on, ending with their family name. They retain their names after marriage, so they do not take their husband's name.

The use of the full name chain that many Arabs use is for official use on documentation only, for example for passports and marriage certificates. Otherwise, it is not necessary to refer to them all.

In correspondence the rules are again variable. Use business cards as a clue.

Some surnames are derived from tribes as a matter of family policy. The root name (i.e. the last name) is often a description of ancestors, a tribal name, or a place.

Example of the derivation of the name string of a male, Ali Abdullah Mughram Al-Ghamdi:

Given name	Father's name	Grandfather's name	Surname, perhaps tribal name
Ali	Abdullah	Mughram	Al-Ghamdi

In general people do not call someone only by their first names except between close social friends. They will always use the honorific before the given name when addressing each other at work. Thus, using the example of the name string above, he would be addressed simply as *Sayid Ali*.

In correspondence it is usual, but not the rule, to use the honorific followed by the given name, father's name, and last name. Thus: *Sayid Ali Abdullah Al-Ghamdi*. Therefore, if any names are to be left out, they should be those sandwiched between the father's name and the final name in the string.

Titles are very important. Therefore in correspondence address an engineer as: *Engineer Ali Al-Ghamdi*. This also applies to lawyers and doctors. Sometimes it may be stretched to include accountants and architects, but there is no firm rule.

In oral address too, use the full professional title. On subsequent mention one should say simply "Engineer", or "Doctor", etc.

There is often no way to distinguish between a married and unmarried women by their names.

When writing to a married woman it is customary with many households to do so via the husband.

A single woman whose name is Taibah Atallah El-Garny would be addressed informally (and orally) by acquaintances as *Miss Taibah*, but formally as *Miss El-Garny*.

In correspondence she would be addressed as *Miss Taibah El-Garny*.

The use of Al signifies "tribe of".

Titles

The word Sheikh, meaning "old man", is an honorific used among the tribes to describe a tribal leader or man of widely accepted distinction.

In the UAE, including Dubai, Sheikh applies to the rulers and leading members of the ruler's families. It therefore denotes royal descent.

A Minister should be addressed as *Maali al Wazir*.

Eastern Caribbean States of
St Christopher and St Nevis, St Lucia, St Vincent and the Grenadines, Anguilla, Montserrat, Dominica.

Mr Richard GUNN

Forms of address in the Eastern Caribbean States are essentially the same as for the UK. However, there is also a Creole oral form of address in St Lucia and the Commonwealth of Dominica. See below for St Lucia, but see separate chapter for Dominica.

Never address anyone as *Mr first name* without the family name. Until informality is clearly satisfactory always use the surname or all names.

There is now a tendency for women to use both their maiden name and their husband's family name upon marriage, in that order, the names thereby becoming double-barrelled names.

In some of the islands, especially Montserrat, people tend to have double-barrelled surnames, in which case address people use them both.

With Creole (on St Lucia) instead of the English use:

Mr = *Messieurs*   Mrs = *Ma* (and sometimes *Madam*)
                    Miss = *Mamselle*

These are oral forms of address only.

Ecuador

Señora Maria Soledad Cordova *de VALENCIA*

See also the chapter on Spanish American forms of address.

Spanish is spoken.

Mr = *Señor*   Mrs = *Señora*   Miss = *Señorita*

In correspondence abbreviate to:

Sr.   Sra.   Srta.

The given name is followed by the father's surname, then the mother's surname. Thus: *Roberto Silva Garcia.*

Address people orally by their first surname. Thus: Señor Silva.

In correspondence, use all names.

In writing, married women use Señora (oral) or Sra. (written) followed by the given name, father's surname, "de" (of), then husband's surname. Orally, one would normally address and refer to a married women by her preferred surname, e.g. *Señora Campora* or *Señora de Campora*. For verbal communication, *Señora Díaz de Campora* is too long. The same applies to unmarried women. *Srta. María García* is too long, so one would tend to say *Srta. García* in conversation.

Use professional titles. An engineer is *Ingeniero/Ingeniera*, a graduate is *Licenciado/Licenciada*, a doctor of medicine is *Doctor/a*. Abbreviate in correspondence to *Ing.*, *Lic.*, and *Dr.* respectively.

Whether writing or speaking, you may use either of these forms of address:

- Place the honorific before the courtesy title. Thus *Señor/a Ingeniero/a Dávalos.*
- Omit the honorific. Thus: *Ingeniero Dávalos.*

Don/Doña is not generally used and some people don't like it. If the situation is very formal and it is appropriate, precede with the honorific. Thus *Señor Don . . .*

There are no hereditary titles.

Some members of the political establishment are addressed as *The Honourable.* Say: *El Honorable Silva.* But write: *Señor Ingeniero Roberto Silva, Honorable Diputado.*

Address an Ambassador by saying: *Señor Embajador.* Write: *Señor Embajador Roberto Silva Garcia.*

Address a Minister by saying: *Señor Ministro.*

Egypt

Al-Sayeda DINA Taha Moussa

Use the following conversationally and for correspondence (before the first name):

Mr = *Al-Sayed*   Mrs = *Al-Sayeda*   Miss = *Al-Anisa*

Always use the *Al-*prefix for correspondence. The prefix may be dropped when addressing the person before you, though it is usually preferable to include it.

The following may also be used conversationally in the same way. Typically, they are used as respectful titles, as for a person who later in life meets with his schoolteacher or professorl. Sometimes *Madame* can be said instead of *Al-Ostaza*, though that is becoming less usual. They are also appropriate for addressing senior colleagues at work. *Al-Ostaza* is a form of address for older unmarried women.

Al-Ostaz   *Al-Ostaza*   *Al Anessa*

Whichever honorific you use, follow it with the given name. Thus: *Al-Ostaz Abdel Aziz* (see below). **Always** use the given name(s).

Example of a name string:

Abdel Aziz / Saleh Eddin / Abdel Aziz
(NB: this name reads as Abdel Aziz Saleh Eddin Abdel Aziz)

Abdel Aziz together comprise the first name, Saleh Eddin is the father's name, and the second Abdel Aziz might be the family name but could also be the grandfather's name.

Many names are compounds, sometimes hyphenated, sometimes not. Recognising when to use them is really a matter of familiarity. As a rule, Abdel will always form part of a compound forename (e.g. Abdel Aziz). Moreover, some names take different forms, such as Saleh Eddin, which might also appear as Saleh El-Din, though this last form would not be used conversationally.

Returning to our name string example, if you don't know whether Abdel Aziz is a man of letters, say *Al-Ostaz Abdel Aziz*. Informally, just say *Abdel Aziz*.

However, with *Al-Sayeda Dina Taha Moussa*, Dina is the first name, Taha is her father's name, and Moussa might be the family name but could also be the grandfather's name. There are no compound names. Say: *Al-Sayeda Dina*.

Women do not take their husband's name upon marriage. Correspondence may be addressed directly to the woman.

The honorific Bek (but say Beh), is used when informally addressing someone to whom you are showing respect. Use this after the first name and before the family name (or sometimes before the second name). Thus: *Abdel Aziz bek Saleh Eddin.* The feminine equivalent is Hanem. These are oral forms of address which are essentially traditional – do not use them in correspondence. They used to be popular but are less so now. One frequently, though not inevitably, places *Al-* beforehand, as with *Al-Bek* and *Al-Hanem.*

The highest respectful title is *Basha* (male only, and sometimes, though not usually, preceded by *Al-*, as in *Al-Basha*). It is not an official title, but is used either alone or with the first name when addressing such personalities as the Prime Minister and government Ministers.

For formal correspondence, open like this:

> Al Sayed (m) Al Ostaz (m) Abdel Aziz Saleh Eddin.
> (And use this style on the envelope)

If he is a doctor, write:

> Al Ostaz Al Doctor Abdel Aziz Saleh Eddin.

When writing to a woman the opening may be either *Al Ostaza* ... or *Al Sayeeda* ...

After writing the name, place the person's *position* underneath (manager, etc), and add at the opening to correspondence:

> Taheya tayebba wa baad (My greetings).

There have been no hereditary titles since 1952.

Professional qualifications:

Doctor = Dr. (Thus: Dr Abdel Aziz, or sometimes: Al-Ostaz Al-Doctor Abdel Aziz).

Accountant (Arabic = Al Mohasseb) – use Ostaz
Architect – use Mohandess
A dentist is Dr.

Lawyers (mohamy, in transliteration from Arabic) are addressed as Al-Ostaz (+ first name), but in correspondence write "lawyer"/ mohamy underneath the name.

An engineer is addressed orally as "Al Mohandess" though in writing "Engineer" will do. An architect, and persons such as computer operators, provided they have a degree, are also addressed as engineers.

The title Sheikh is still applied mainly to those wearing formal Islamic dress and some tribal elders, and to the chief of any of the desert tribes. It is always used when addressing anyone of high religious learning.

Hag (m and f) precedes the first name of those who have been to Mecca, as with *Hag Dina*. It is not used in correspondence.

Summary of preferential forms

Depending upon the degree of respect that is appropriate, use the following (which are in ascending order of prominence). Explanations are given above. Also note from the above text when to use or omit the use of the *Al-* prefix.

- Al-Sayed   Al-Sayeda   Al-Anessa
- Al-Ostaz   Al-Ostaza   Al-Anessa
- Bek   Hanim
- Basha

El Salvador

Dr Mauricio ROSALES-Rivera

SPANISH IS SPOKEN.

Mr = *Señor*   Mrs = *Señora*   Miss = *Señorita*

In correspondence abbreviate to:

Sr.   Sra.   Srta.

The given name is followed by the father's surname, then the mother's surname. Use the honorific followed by the father's surname. Thus: *Doctor Rosales* (or *Señor Rosales*, if appropriate).

In writing, married women use Señora followed by the given name, father's surname, *de* (of), then their husband's surname. Thus: *Señora Lilian Concepción Laguardia de Rosales.* Orally, one would normally address and refer to a married women by her preferred surname, e.g. *Señora Campora* or *Señora de Campora.* For verbal communication, *Señora Díaz de Campora* is too long. The same applies to unmarried women. *Srta. María García* is too long, so one would tend to say *Srta. García* in conversation.

When writing, use all names, whether to men or women.

For persons of rank: *Señor Ministro* (Minister). His Excellency the Ambassador should be addessed as *Su Excelencia* – followed by forename(s) and family name.

The courtesy titles *Don* and *Doña* are used for eminent persons. Say: *Señor Don* (m) or *Señora Doña* (f) followed by the given name. Thus: *Señor Don Luis.*

There are no hereditary or conferred titles.

Professional titles: Someone with a degree in engineering is called *Ingeniero* (m)/*Ingeniera* (f), and someone with a university degree in any subject at post graduate level is a *Licenciado* (m)/*Licenciada* (f). A medical doctor or person with a doctorate in any discipline is a *Doctor/a.* In oral address use the professional title followed by the father's surname. Thus: Dr. Dominguez.

In correspondence use *Ing., Lic., Dr.,* respectively, but begin with the professional title followed by the given name, then the father's surname, then the mother's surname. Thus: Dr. Orlando Morales García.

Whether writing or speaking it is optional whether or not to place the honorific before the courtesy title, as with: Sr. Ing. Rosales.

Equatorial Guinea

Señor Daniel José EDJANG Ngueme

SPANISH IS SPOKEN. USE SPANISH FORMS OF ADDRESS.

Mr = *Señor*   Mrs = *Señora*   Miss = Señorita

But write:

Sr.   Sra.   Srta.

For ordinary situations the following examples should be sufficient. Follow the honorific with the father's family name. Thus: Señor Edjang.

Please refer to chapter on Spain for further details.

Eritrea

Ato GHEBREMICHAEL Mengistu

Mr = *Ato*   Mrs = *Woizero*   Miss = Woizerit

Tegregna and Arabic are two of the five most used languages in Eritrea. UK forms of address are widely acceptable.

There are no family names and people are addressed by the honorific preceding their first name.

Women retain their maiden names upon marriage, and are also addressed by their first name. Thus LUUL Kahsay is addressed as Woizero LUUL.

Estonia

Härra Riivo SINIJARV

Mr = *Härra*　　　Mrs = *Proua*　　　Miss = *Preili*

There are no patronymic names and there is no Russian influence any more. Under Soviet rule it was commonplace to refer to the family name first, but this is no longer so. First names and surnames are now in the customary Western order, with the given name followed by the surname.

Written and oral forms of address are the same.

There are no hereditary or conferred titles.

Ethiopia

Mr WAHIDE Belay

Use Mr, Mrs, and Miss, but apply the honorific to the first name only. Thus *Musa Elmi Ali* would be addressed as *Mr Musa*.

Women always retain their family names upon marriage. They should therefore be referred to separately.

Falkland Islands

Forms of address correspond to those used in the UK.

Fiji

Mrs Luisa WAGANIKA

Forms of address in Fiji are the same as for the UK.

Although Fiji is a republic without a royal family, appropriate forms of address are retained for those who were of royal descent.

A Prince enjoys the honorific "Ratu", and a Princess is addressed as "Adi". Place these honorifics before the surname. All Chiefs in Fiji are of Royal lineage and are therefore also to be addressed like this.

Finland

Herra Ilkka HIIRSALMI

Mr = *Herra*   Mrs = *Rouva*   Miss = *Neiti*

In correspondence abbreviate to:

Hra.   *Rva.*   *Nti.*

There is no equivalent to the Western use of Ms but there is now a trend emerging for it to be adopted in informal correspondence. The English letters *Ms* are then used.

In common with most Western countries, the forename is followed by the family name. Thus: Matti Mäkinen would be addressed as *Herra Matti Mäkinen*.

France

Monsieur Philippe PERRIER

Monsieur, Madame, and Mademoiselle, followed by the forename and surname, or by just the surname, are used in writing and in speech. Thus: *Monsieur Perrier*.

Mr = *Monsieur*   Mrs = *Madame*   Miss = *Mademoiselle*

In correspondence abbreviate to:

M   *Mme*   *Mlle*

Use of an equivalent for the English Ms has not evolved in French society, which remains inclined towards formality.

Do not abbreviate when corresponding with a titled person, use the complete form.

Monsieur, Madame, and Mademoiselle may be used in speech to everyone, whatever their status, when engaged in conversation.

In correspondence:

M = *Monsieur*
MM = *Messieurs*
Mme = *Madame*

Mlle = *Mademoiselle*
Mlles = *Mademoiselles*
Mgr = Monseigneur
Me = *Maître*
Mes = *Maîtres*
Dr = *Docteur*
Drs = *Docteurs*

A lawyer is addressed as *Maître* (then family name).

Anybody with a PhD is addressed as *Docteur* (then family name). In correspondence doctors are addressed as *Monseiur* (or Madame etc) *family name, Docteur en* (followed by "médecine", or appropriate achievement).

The honorific comes before all appointments and names. Thus, in oral address, say: *Monsieur le docteur.*

An ambassador is addressed as *Votre Excellence.* Use *Son Excellence* if writing about an Ambassador.

An officer of the armed forces is addressed by men, in writing and in speech, as (for instance) *Mon Colonel*, or *Mon Général*, but by women as *Colonel*, or Général.

The wives of generals, colonels, etc are often referred to colloquially by their husbands' rank. Thus: *Madame la Générale.* The correct form is Madame (family name).

Once ennobled with a title, the entire family is entitled to benefit in perpetuity as well as their descendants. No-one in the family, however junior, is a commoner.

In general, all sons and daughters are known by the family title also.

When addressing persons with titles, employees and servants would use the oral form "Madame la marquise" etc. So a Duke or Duchess is addressed as Monsieur le duc or Madame la duchesse.

The formal opening of a letter to a titled person should begin (for example): *Monsieur le duc*. It should be signed off with: Je vous prie d'agréer, Monsieur le duc, l'expression de mes sentiments respectueux...

Titles are still conferred. Some principal titles:

Prince de (Princesse de)
Duc de (Duchesse de)
Marquis de (Marquise de)
Comte de (Comtesse de)
Vicomte de (Vicomtesse de)
Baron de (Baronne de)

Gabon

Madame Manna NGONDET

French forms of address apply. The family name appears last.

Monsieur, Madame, and Mademoiselle, followed by the forename and surname, or by just the surname, are used in writing and in speech, where Monsieur, Madame, and Mademoiselle are Mr, Mrs and Miss respectively. Thus: *Monsieur Ngondet*.

Women adopt their husband's family name upon marriage.

There are neither hereditary nor conferred titles.

French is the binding language for villages that speak different dialects.

The Gambia

Mr Momodou JUWARA

The Gambia follows UK custom, with the family name appearing last.

It has been the tradition for women to retain their maiden names upon marriage and continue to be addressed as "Miss", but this convention is changing. Many women now prefer to be addressed as "Mrs" followed by their husband's family name.

Male Muslims who have been to Mecca precede their names with *Al Haji*, women use *Al Haja*.

The head of a village is addressed as *Alkalo* followed by his full name or family name.

Similarly, the head of a district is addressed as *Chief* followed by his full name or family name.

There is some French influence, but it is informal. Forms of address are essentially English.

Georgia

Batoni GIORGI Sulkashvili

The patronymic system and the use of a second name that were widespread under Russian rule have been abandoned.

Address people by the honorific followed by the first name only, as with *Mr Giorgi* (though you may, if you wish, use both names). The use of the family name (Sulkashvili) instead of the given name would be very formal. It is the same rule for women.

Mr = *Batoni*   Mrs = *Kalbatoni*   Miss = *Kalbatoni*

For correspondence, Kalbatoni is the equivalent to Ms, so should be used whenever writing to a woman. When orally addressing an unmarried woman, say *Kalbatoni* alone (without the name).

Just as in speech, in correspondence the use of the honorific with the family name (second name) would usually be considered too formal. Use the first name only.

Name forms often indicate the region from which the person comes. For instance, someone whose name ends with *-shvili* would probably come from East or central Georgia (it means *son or daughter of*), names ending with *-ua* are probably from Western Georgia, and those ending wth *-iani* or *-uri* are probably from the mountainous regions.

Germany

Frau Christa WINKLER

Oral forms of address for commoners are Herr (Mr) and Frau (Mrs) followed by the family name. Thus: Hans Peter Gruber would be addressed as *Herr Gruber*.

Women up to the age of about 18 *used to be* addressed as Fräulein, thereafter as Frau. Modern custom is to address all women as Frau, even teenagers. Therefore *Frau* does not necessarily indicate marriage.

When addressing professional persons, people with rank, and government ministers, precede the title with the honorific. Thus: *Herr Minister, Herr Doktor, Frau Professor* – followed by the family name. However, it is no longer customary to refer to the spouse by the title.

Titles of nobility are an integral part of the name, and the forename is used before the title when addressing the envelope. It is no longer customary to place Herr or Frau in front. Thus the count Manfred (von) Bodman would be: *Manfred Graf (von) Bodman*. His wife would be similarly addressed, using *Gräfin*. *Komtesse* is the appropriate title for an unmarried daughter of a count. Open correspondence as follows: Sehr geehrter [Dear] Graf . . . (omitting the *von*).

Those with hereditary titles are addressed as *Graf* followed by the seat, which becomes part of the name. Thus: *Graf Hochburg* (oral) would be addressed in writing like this: *Dr. Hans Wilhelm Graf von Hochburg*.

Baron, in place of the title *Freiherr* (m), is used extensively in South Germany. Orally and in writing it should be *Baron von* . . . or, *Herr von* . . . A *Baroness* (f) is the unmarried daughter of the *Baron*, and his wife is a *Baronin*. It is no longer necessary to use these titles expansively for oral forms of address. For instance, instead of *Herr Freiherr von Bodman*, say *Herr (von) Bodman* or say *Baron (von) Hochburg*. Note that the use of *von* is now optional too.

Titles are borne by sons and unmarried daughters before their forenames. They are not retained by daughters who marry outside the nobility.

Titles:

Prince – *Prinz*
Princess – *Prinzessin*
Count – *Graf*
Countess – *Gräfin*
Duke – *Herzog*
Duchess – *Herzogin*
Baron – *Freiherr/Baron*
Baroness – *Freifrau/Baronin*

GHANA

Mr Emmanuel KWAMI

Forms of address generally follow UK custom, but there are tribal influences.

Informally, address people by their first name. More formally, use their family name, which appears last. Thus: *Mr James Kwamena ANAMAN*.

Women usually adopt their husband's family name upon marriage.

The tribal Chiefs are addressed with due formality, but there are several dialects. Foreigners are often expected to follow local custom by addressing the Chiefs in their dialect.

With the majority Akan group, which uses the Twi dialect, the chief is addressed as *Nana*, followed by his "stool" name, followed by his family name. The stool name is an adopted name earned after a test of valour. There may be several clans, so the chiefs rotate. Thus: *Nana Otumfuo* (+ family name).

The Akan group use the following forms of address:

Mr = *Owura*   Mrs (and Miss) = *Awura*

In the Accra region (which uses the Ta dialect) you should say *Nii* instead of *Nana*; in the Volta region say *Togbe*; and in the Northern region say *Naa*.

There are no particular forms of address for persons with professional qualifications.

Gibraltar

Forms of address correspond to those used in the UK.

Do not use Spanish forms of address.

Greece

Kyrios Angelos M. Angelides.

Forms of address are equivalent to UK custom, with family names appearing last for speech and social correspondence. Note that all nouns are declinable.

For official correspondence, such as in government departments, banks, large organisations, etc, place the family name first, then the given name. Note that *Angelos Angelides* would therefore become *Angelides Angelos*.

Mr = *Kyrios*   Mrs = *Kyria*   Miss = *Despoinida*.

Abbreviate Kyrios to k. (small k) in correspondence. Thus: *k. Angelides*. (An alternative abbreviation is, as it most often appears, kon; as this form declines, it is best avoided by non-Greek speakers). similarly, abbreviate Kyria to Ka, as with *Ka Angelides*. Abbreviate Despoinida to Dis. Thus: *Dis Angelides*.

There is no equivalent to the use of Ms.

As a general rule of translation, transliteration of Greek words is only used in English where a translation does not exist. Where there is an equivalent word in English (as *Mr* for *k.*), the English form is preferable (so: *Mr Angelos Angelides, or Mr A. Angelides*). Also in some instances where there is an English equivalent for certain first names, like Constantine for Constantinos, George for Giorgos, John for Yiannis, etc., use of the English name is quite acceptable and often preferable.

Women tend to adopt their husband's family name upon marriage, but not always. There is now an inclination to hyphenate the maiden name to the husband's.

It is usual for a person's name to include their father's initial in the middle. Thus: *Constantine T. Voliotis.*

Uneducated people tend to say, for example, *Mrs Firstname*, but it is incorrect. One should properly use the honorific before the family name.

There are no titles of nobility.

Grenada

Mr Ashley David ALEXANDER

Forms of address in Grenada are the same as for the UK.

Guadaloupe

Forms of address are the same as for France. See the chapter on France for more details.

Mr = *Monsieur*   Mrs = *Madame*   Miss = *Mademoiselle*

Guam and The Marianas

English is the official language, though Japanese and Chamorro are also spoken.

Forms of address are used as in American English.

Guatemala

Señor Carlos Oswaldo CÁCERES Vittorazzi

Spanish is spoken.

Mr = *Señor*   Mrs = *Señora*   Miss = *Señorita*

In correspondence abbreviate to:

Sr.   *Sra.*   *Srta.*

People retain both their father's and mother's surnames. Thus: Señor Juan Alfredo Vargas Domínguez, where *Juan Alfredo* are given names, *Vargas* is the family name of the father and *Domínguez* is that of the mother. Address him as Señor Vargas.

Where the woman's name is, for example, Jane Vargas de Domínguez, address her as *Señora de Domínguez*.

Persons with rank or position should be addressed like this:

Señor Ministro (Minister),
Señor Embajador (Ambassador).

Graduates and professional people are addressed, for instance, as Ingeniero (m) / Ingeniera (f) and Licenciado (m) / Licenciada (f) respectively. Orally, it is unnecessary to place the honorific beforehand, but when writing it is optional, though in practice one should use both on more formal occasions.

There are no conferred or hereditary titles.

The following appears after the family name on the envelope:

Ing. (for Ingeniero, an engineer).
Lic. (for Licenciado, a person with a general degree).
Doctors and persons with PhDs should always be addressed as Doctor (m) / Doctora (f).

Remember that people are offended if their degrees are not noted.

The courtesy titles *Don* (m) and *Doña* (f) are used before the Christian name when showing respect. Thus: *Don Juan*. It is no longer customary to place the honorific beforehand.

Formal signing off of letters:

Me suscribo de Usted atentamente = Yours faithfully
Le saluda atentamente = Yours sincerely

Guiana, French

FRENCH AND CREOLE FRENCH ARE SPOKEN.

Forms of address are the same as for France. See the chapter on France for more details.

Mr = *Monsieur*   Mrs = *Madame*   Miss = *Mademoiselle*

Guinea

Madame Aissata SOW-DIALLO

Mr = *Monsieur*   Mrs = *Madame*   Miss = *Mademoiselle*

French forms of address are acceptable (see chapter on France).

Some women hyphenate their maiden name to their husband's family name upon marriage, as in the above example.

Address a company director as *Monsieur le directeur*, and a government Minister as *Monsieur le ministre*.

Guinea-Bissau

Senhor Óscar Batica FERREIRA

Portuguese is spoken. Use Portuguese forms of address.

Mr = *Senhor*   Miss / Mrs = *Senhora*

Address people formally by their last name, thus: *Senhor Ferreira*.

Guyana

Mr Kenneth Aloysius ABDELNOUR

The official language is English though Creole English is used in the country areas and is the most widely used vernacular. This has no effect, however, on forms of address, which are in standard English throughout the country.

Forms of address in Guyana are the same as for the UK.

Haiti

Misier Jean CASIMIR

The language is Créole, with a small elite and the ruling caste speaking high French. Créole has been the official language since 1987 and comprises a mixture of terms and forms derived from Spanish, English, African dialects, and French. The French element itself evolves from the 17th and 18th century. Créole is therefore a curious cocktail that is a language in its own right rather than a dialect.

Forms of address correspond largely to those of France, but the spelling (and the pronunciation) is different:

Mr = *Misier*   Mrs/Miss = *Madan*

Mademoiselle is not used.

How are you = *Qui manieu*

City people are addressed by the last name (family name) of their name string, but in the countryside people address one another by their first names.

Women acquire their husband's family name upon marriage.

Honduras

Señora Lilian Maria Vargas Domínguez *de ZERON*

See also the chapter on Spanish forms of address.

<small>SPANISH IS SPOKEN.</small>

<small>MR</small> = *SEÑOR*   <small>MRS</small> = *SEÑORA*   <small>MISS</small> = *SEÑORITA*

In correspondence abbreviate to:

Sr.   *Sra.*   *Srta.*

People retain the surnames of both their father and mother. Thus: *Señor Juan Alfredo Vargas Domínguez*, where *Juan Alfredo* are given names, *Vargas* is the family name of the father and *Domínguez* is that of the mother.

Where the woman's name is, for example, Jane Vargas de Domínguez, address her as *Señora de Domínguez*, or *Señora Domínguez*.

Persons with rank or position should be addressed like this:

Señor Ministro (Minister).
Señor Embajador (Ambassador).

Graduates and professional people are addressed, for instance, as Ingeniero (m) / Ingeniera (f) and Licenciado (m) / Licenciada (f) respectively. When writing place the honorific beforehand. Thus: Sr. Lic. Vargas. But omit the honorific in conversation. Thus: Licenciado Vargas.

It is customary to address a professional person by his/her title, particularly on the first meeting or on early acquaintance. Most graduates, for instance, are *Licenciados*, but other common titles are *Doctor* (m) and *Doctora* (f), and *Ingeniero*.

When writing to someone who is a *Licenciado*, close your letter with: Me subscribo de Usted como su átento servidor (or Atentamente).

Don and *Doña* are used for addressing distinguished personalities, but do not use them with the honorific. Use one or the other.

Correspondence in Spanish follows a formal style. Address Ministers as *Excelentísimo Señor Ministro*, and refer to him/her in the body of the document as V.E. (Vuestra Excelencia). The letter should close with: Me subscribo del Señor Ministro como su átento y seguro servidor.

The Head of State is addressed as *Su Excelencia*. Government Ministers are *Excelentísimo*, but after introducing oneself it is usual to say merely *Señor Ministro*.

Hong Kong

Mr WANG Zhizhuang

The family name precedes the given name. Thus Zhu Zushou should be addressed as *Mr Zhu*, and Gu Jingxian would be *Madame* (or Mrs.) *Gu*. When informality is appropriate, address them as *Zushou* and *Jingxian* respectively. This is usually acceptable after an introductory meeting.

In Hong Kong, Chinese family names are often mono-syllables and given names usually comprise double syllables or two compound syllables. This differs from countries such as Singapore, where most Chinese separate their names into three distinct monosyllables, though still beginning with the family name.

As Hong Kong has been a British dependency, there are conferred titles (such as a knighthood). British citizens living in Hong Kong are addressed as they would be in the UK. Chinese people are addressed this way, so that, for instance, *Chung Sze-yuen*, who has a knighthood, is addressed as *Sir Sze-yuen*. Some titled Chinese may elect to drop their titles after China takes over in 1997.

See also the note on dialects under China.

Hungary

NAGY András úr

There was some Germanic influence on forms of address during the 19th century and early 20th century. Nowadays Hungary adopts a polite mode, modern, and without too much ceremony. However, it remains somewhat complex.

The honorific follows the name, and the family name appears as the first name in the name string.

Thus: *SZABÓ Judit* (where Judit is the given name).

Mr = *úr* Thus: Mr András NAGY (as he would be addressed in the UK) is addressed as NAGY András úr.

Mrs = *né* Thus: Mrs András NAGY is addressed as NAGY Andrásné (with "né" suffixed to the given name).

Miss = *kisasszony* Thus: Miss Katalin NAGY is addressed as NAGY Katalin kisasszony.

Family names are always used and have only one form. They are not affected by honorifics.

Oral and written forms of address remain the same for unmarried women. They may be addressed by their given name. Thus: SZABÓ

Judit is an unmarried woman who can be called either SZABÓ kisasszony, or just *Judit*.

Formal opening for correspondence:

Tisztelt (name) úr! (Mr) *or*, without name: Tisztelt Uram!

Tisztelt (name) Asszony! (Mrs) *or*, without name: Tisztelt Asszonyom!

Tisztelt (name) Kisasszony! (Miss) *or*, without name: Tisztelt Kisasszony!

Sign off: Tisztelettel (Yours Truly).

Professional persons are addressed orally like this:

doktor úr (medicine, or lawyer)
mérnök úr (engineer)

In written form this becomes (formally): *dr NAGY András úr*, or (informally) dr NAGY András. A professor is written to simply as *prof. NAGY*.

Hereditary titles are very rarely used. However, there are some forms in use. The title is followed by the surname and given names. For instance, the written form of address for Count István Széchenyi is: *Gróf* SZÉCHENYI István. A Countess is addressed as grófné.

In oral address, Count becomes *gróf úr*, and a Countess is still *grófné*.

There are no conferred titles.

Persons of rank should be addressed orally like this:

Mr Minister, represented as: miniszter úr
Mr MP : képviseló úr
Mr Ambassador : nagykövet úr

When writing, the name and rank is followed by the honorific. Thus: H.E. András NAGY, ambassador = NAGY András úr öexcellenciája.

If he is an MP address him as:

NAGY András képsiveló úr.

Iceland

Herra LEIFUR Eiriksson
Frú PORDIS Haraldsdottir

Mr = *Herra*   Mrs = Frú   Miss = *Fröken*

In correspondence abbreviate to:

Hr.   *Fru.*   *Fruk.*

There is no oral equivalent to Ms, but, as in Denmark, the abbreviation Fr. is used in correspondence for either Frú or Fröken.

Patronymics are employed.

Most Icelanders derive their last name from their father's first name. Thus: *Leifur Eiriksson* is the son of *Eirikur*, of which *Eiriksson* is the derivative.

Similarly, a woman named Pordis Haraldsdottir has the given name *Pordis* and the family name *Haraldsdottir* which is derived from her father, *Harald*.

If Pordis Haraldsdottir marries Leifur Eiriksson she does not become Eiriksson. She continues to be Pordis Haraldsdottir.

If Pordis and Leifur have a son, he would have Leifsson as a last name. Similarly, a daughter would have Leifsdottir as her last name.

Eiriksson, Leifsson, and Haraldsdottir are not regarded as true surnames. Icelanders therefore prefer to be addressed by their given names. The patronymic is never used alone.

This practice also applies when addressing persons with standing in the community. The recent President of Iceland, Vigdis Finnboga-dottir, would be addressed by both names, or as President Vigdis, but *never* as President Finnbogadottir.

There are a limited number of Icelanders who have family names in the usual way.

India

Shri Krishna Venekatachalan RAJAN

See also the introductory chapter on Indian names.

There are more than 700 dialects in India, but UK custom is widely acceptable and Mr, Mrs, and Miss are routinely used, especially by the business community. However, the following (Hindi) vocabulary is also recommended, and at least 50% of the population will understand:

Mr = *Shri*   Mrs = *Shrimati*   Miss = *Kumari*

The given name(s) is followed by the family name, as in the West.

Caste

Though the Hindu Caste system has no direct influence on forms of address, surnames may identify a person's caste or locale, and those of the highest caste are often addressed differently. There are four castes in North India to which this applies:

Brahmins, who are scholars or priests, are the highest caste and are often (though not essentially) addressed as *Pundit*, as with *Pundit Nehru*. *Pundit* is used before the first name, or before the last name if it has been abbreviated (see the separate chapter on Indian names), though there is no firm rule. Only male Brahmins are addressed this way; women are addressed as described above. It is also acceptable to address male Brahmins – indeed everybody who is male – as *Shri*.

The second caste are Kshatriyas (warriors). If they belong to a "princely family" specific honorifics apply, but for general and practical purposes their names end with Singh and they are addressed as *Sardar* (masc.) or *Sardarnee* (fem., for Miss/Mrs) instead of Shri / Shrimati Kumari.

The third caste are Vaishya (traders). Ordinary forms of address apply.

The fourth caste are Shudra (untouchables). Ordinary forms of address apply.

Juniors apply the honorific Ji (meaning *heart*, but used as an honorific) when addressing senior male or female Hindus. It is an informal but respectful Hindustani form of oral address that is more widely used in the North of India though understood everywhere. Sometimes it is placed after the family name, and sometimes after the first name. "Cha cha Ji" ("dear uncle"), is also used informally when juniors address male seniors, where "uncle" is applied as a general term of endearment regardless of relationship.

A male teacher or holy man is addressed as *Guru*. This covers the full educational spectrum of schools and universities, as well as "mentors". This form of respectful address originated for use with teachers and evolved later for use with priests. *Guru* may precede the first name or the last name, there is no rule. An enhanced form of respect is to address such a person as *Guru Ji* (before their name, as described).

Learned scholars are addressed as *Acharya* instead of *Guru*.

There are also specific forms of address used within the family to denote respect when addressing one another. For instance, *Aap* (respect-word, gender neutral) precedes the first name when speaking to an elder, and *Tum* (meaning *you*, gender neutral), when the elder addresses the younger.

Professional qualifications are not added to names except for medical practitioners (use Dr.)

There are no longer any hereditary titles and ordinary forms of address are used when greeting those with conferred titles.

Persons of position are addressed orally as *Sir* or *Madam* but in correspondence the customary *Dear Sir* or *Dear Madam* is sufficient.

Ambassadors are addressed as *His/Her Excellency*, and Ministers as *Honourable Minister* (Oral) or *Hon'able Minister* (Written).

Sahib (Sir) and Ma'am Sahib (Madame) are used sometimes, usually when addressing a foreigner, and are placed after the family name: *Tully Sahib*.

Note: In Indian languages tones and forms of address are often used to ask nicely and receive politely instead of specific words such as please or thank you. This sometimes results in the omission of such niceties when English is used there.

Indonesia

If in doubt use the FIRST NAME
Thus: Bapak ZAINAL Arifin

Introductions can become complicated because there are many titles and long names, though there are also people who have only one name, such as President Suharto.

With 336 ethnic groups, there are many clues to a person's origin in his name. The Javanese comprise the largest group, but the Dayaks of Kalimantan, the Bataks of Sumatra, and the Bugis of Sulawesi, are also prominent.

There are usually no family names. Men and women are known by their given name(s) followed by their father's name.

For formal introductions you should begin with Bapak or Ibu (Sir or Madam, where Ibu is the equivalent of Ms. Both are well-suited for addressing everyone), followed by any academic or professional title, then the person's given names. If the person has a noble title, it precedes the given name.

Conversationally, Bapak is often abbreviated to *Pak* and Ibu to *Bu*.

Nyonya (Mrs) tends to be used instead of *Ibu* when Indonesians address foreigners, for instance if you are a businessman accompanied by your wife. It is also sometimes used between Indonesians. But the preference is usually for *Ibu*, especially between Indonesians.

In correspondence, Nyonya is shortened to *Ny*.

Women adopt their husband's name for official purposes upon marriage (such as for passports). Otherwise they do not usually do so, though there are many exceptions as there is no firm rule. When wives do adopt their husband's name, it is the first name of the name string.

Here are some examples of forms of address:

Zainal Arifin has no family name. Both names are given. Indonesians tend to have anything from a solitary name to as many as four given names. Zainal Arifin is *Bapak* (Mr) *ZAINAL*, but will not mind if you call him *Bapak Arifin*. His wife, if she takes his name, is *Ibu Zainal* (Mrs Zainal).

However, *Sahala Manumpak Panggabean* is addressed as Bapak *Panggabean* befcause Panggabean is a Batakness from North Sumatra and his last name is his tribal name. His close friends would call him *Sahala*. Some other popular names to which this formula applies are: Siregar, Sihombing, Manlirung, Silalahi.

There is no difficulty knowing how to address Mr Soerpardijono, who has only one name.

Bali

Balinese people in particular can have names passed down through the generations, but it may be the first name, the second name, etc. There is no established rule of order, and they are not family names. Moreover, the names may shift in order with each generation.

In Bali each name has symbolic significance, denoting order and importance within the community. This caste system allows commoners to have "nonsense words" (or inventions) for names, whilst the gentry often use Sanskrit. There are apparently also occasions when the order of names is changed to mislead evil spirits.

Java

Long Javanese and Sundanese names may be abbreviated in conversation only.

As a general rule Indonesians tend to use only one of their names and you should say *Bapak* (or *Ibu*) followed by that name. If in doubt use the first name.

But in correspondence use the whole name, even for an informal letter. Sign off your letters with "Hormat Saya" (Yours Very Truly).

Note also that *Ibu* is used for women of rank and position (instead of Nyonya). Men are always *Bapak*.

Children just have given names and usually have also a nickname for use only among family.

In Central and East Java most first names end with -*o*, as with Cipto Mangunkusumo. People from Sunda (which is West Java) are typically identifiable by repetition of the final syllable, as with Ir*man* Sueri*man*, or Irwan Mulia*wan*, or by having a name ending with -*a*, as with Purwakarta.

East Timor

Timorese citizens usually have names of Portuguese origin, such as Abilio Jose Osorio Soares, who would be addressed as Mr Soares. However, instead of Portuguese honorifics, *Bapak* and *Ibu* are used.

Chinese community

Chinese characters are not allowed to be used in Indonesia. The Chinese community adopt Indonesian names though some business-men also use their Chinese names, spelt phonetically in English. Their business card should help identify how to address them.

Some Chinese adopt local names which include their Chinese name. Thus LIM Siaw Liong might become Isadano Sa*lim*. Similarly, the popular Chinese family name *Tan* is concealed within Irwan Su*tan*to.

Professional titles

Although there is Dutch influence, this has no real consequence on forms of address except for persons of academic standing. Indeed, the use of academic titles derives from the Dutch. Such titles are important and should precede the given name.

Drs. applies to a male graduate of any field except engineering or law. *Dra* is the female equivalent.

Ir. stands for *Insinjur*, the title for any graduate of engineering.

S Econ, SH, and SS are for Sarjuna Ekonomi, Hukum, and Sastra respectively. These are graduates (or graduands) in economics, law, and letters.

Persons with professional degrees retain the use of their letters in formal correspondence. When writing, address Zainal Arifin, a person with a degree, as:

Ir. Zainal Arifin when he is an engineer.

Prof. Drs. Ir. Zainal when he is a Professor of Engineering

Drs. Zainal M.Sc. when he has a doctorate in another science.

Zainal Arifin SH when he is a lawyer (note the letters SH appear after the name).

Members of Parliament are addressed as Bapak / Ibu.

A Minister is addressed orally as *Bapak Menteri* (followed by the ministry or his/her name). In correspondence use *Menteri Negara* followed (usually) by his/her FIRST name. However, B. J. Habibie, a Minister, is the exception to the rule because he is a Bugis (a tribe from the Menado region of North Sulawesi, in the Celebes). Habibie is his tribal name.

Iran

Agha Gholamreza ANSARI

IN FARSI:

$$Mr = Agha \qquad Mrs/Miss = Khanom$$

The given name is followed by the family name. Thus: Agha Hasam TEHRANI.

There are no hereditary titles.

In correspondence, precede the family name with the professional title. Thus: *Engineer Tehrani.*

There are religious titles. *Ayatollah* is the highest, as with *Ayatollah Seyed Ali Khamenei* (referred to as *Ayatollah Khamenei*). Next, in terms of rank, is *Hojat-ol-Islam* (followed by family name).

Women may choose to take their husband's name, though their maiden name remains on official documents.

Note that Iranians are not Arabs, so Arab forms of address have no influence.

Iraq

Sayed ALI Al-Ghamdi

See also the chapter on Arab names.

Within the name string everyone usually has a given name followed by their father's given name.

Mr = *Sayed*   Mrs/Miss = *Sayeda*

Some surnames are derived from tribes. The root name (i.e.: last name) is often a description of ancestors, a tribal name, or a place.

In correspondence it is usual, but not the rule, to use the honorific followed by the given (the first) name. If any names are to be omitted, they should be those sandwiched between the father's name and the final name in the name string.

Titles are very important. Therefore in correspondence address an engineer as: *Engineer Ali Al-Ghamdi*. This applies also to lawyers and doctors, but bear in mind there is no firm rule. In oral address too, use the full professional title, though on subsequent mention one may say simply "Engineer", or "Doctor".

Women tend to be called by their husband's family name upon marriage. However, some are known in English as, for instance, *Mrs Al-Ghamdi*, whilst others prefer to be *Miss Al-Ghamdi*.

Ireland

Mr Thomas KELLY

Ireland is served by English for general forms of address, but in the political arena use the following:

The Prime Minister is addressed as *Taoiseach* and referred to as *An Taoiseach* (where *An* is the definite article).

The Deputy PM is addressed as *Tánaiste*.

Members of Parliament are TDs (Teachta Dála).

The Speaker of the Upper House is the Cathaoirleach.

The Speaker of the Lower House is the Ceann Comhairle.

The Deputy Speaker of the Lower House is the Leas-Cheann Comhairle.

There are no hereditary or conferred titles in ireland, though there are Anglo-Irish families with English titles.

Israel

Gideon MEIR

It would be a challenge to offend an Israeli with an erroneous form of address. Cast formality aside, honorifics are largely forsaken.
Shalom (peace) is used by everyone to everyone as a greeting, like *Hello*.

The family name appears *last*. Usually, despite the cosmopolitan nature of the population, names are constructed much like those in other Western countries. Some people hyphenate their family names to their spouse's family name, a practice that is slowly evolving and applies sometimes to men too. In those circumstances, ask which name to use.

Orally you may wish, if you want to, use *Mr* or *Mrs* for a first time introduction, but thereafter don't bother. Just use the first name. Exceptionally, and for formal occasions, use *Mar* (before surname) for Mr and *Geveret* for Madam / Mrs or Miss, but revert to informality on second mention.

The informality extends to almost everyone, including government ministers, who may also be addressed by their first names. Otherwise you may be regarded as being rather pompous.

Don't use *Miss* to distinguish an unmarried woman. Just use her first name.

In correspondence you may open with *Dear Mr Meir*, but a simple *Dear Gideon* is perfectly acceptable. It is customary to write the opening of a letter in longhand. Thus: Write "Dear Gideon", then type the letter as usual.

The exception to this liberal eccentricity is when addressing Rabbis, whose salutation, both orally and in correspondence, is *Rabbi* followed by the family name (last name).

Frequently business cards give the surname followed by the first names, a custom established by the military.

There are no conferred or hereditary titles.

Italy

Signor Francesco VILLARI

Mr = *Signor*   Mrs = *Signora*   Miss = *Signorina*

These forms of address may also be used conversationally without a name following. However, when used alone *Signor* becomes *Signore*, with pronunciation of the "e".

Persons with degrees usually retain them in correspondence. A person with a law degree has *Avvocato* before their name. An engineer has *Ingegnere* (abbreviate to *Ing.* in correspondence), an accountant has *Ragioniere* (abbreviate to *Rag.* in correspondence) and an architect has *Architetto*. An elementary school-teacher is addressed as *Maestro* (m) or *Maestra* (f); a teacher at junior school level (11 years plus) is addressed as *Professore/Professoressa*. When used orally, use together with either the Christian name (first name) or the family name (last name). In correspondence, use with the family name.

In correspondence the usual name order is *reversed* so that the surname is followed by the given names. Thus: ROSSI Mario Antonio, but this does not apply to vocal forms of address.

Conversationally, all graduates, especially people with professional degrees, tend to be addressed as *Dottore* (used alone), but the "e" at the end of Dottore (and the "e" at the end of Signore) are dropped when used with a name, as with Dottor ROSSI.

Specifically, people with Ba and BSc degrees are called Dottore (m) or Dottoressa (f). Those with higher degrees (master's) are called Professore (m) or Professoressa (f). Those with medical degrees or PhDs are called *Dottor(e)* or Dottoressa.

In a society where titles play such an important role, when in doubt, call everyone Dottore (m) or Dottoressa (f). Those who are not entitled will also be flattered and it will do no harm.

All courtesy titles may be used alone, thus: "I feel awful, Dottore". However, until there is a measure of familiarity it is recommended that you use the courtesy title with the family name.

Correspondence to professional people should begin with *Egregio* followed by the title and surname, as with *Egregio Dottor Rossi*. Sign off using "Distinti saluti" if formal, or "Cordiali saluti" if familiar.

Titles were abolished in 1947 and no longer have official status. They are, however, still used socially, and are usually used as an accessory to the surname.

There are countless titles: below are some of the most important. Many are bestowed as honours (and they might have been bought). For instance, a director of a successful company may be bestowed with a *Cavaliere del Lavoro* (abbreviate to *Cav.* in correspondence), which becomes a title that is expected to be used as a form of address. Others may be bestowed for political favours with an *Onorevole* (abbreviate to *On.* in correspondence). These titles may be used alone in speech, or with the family name, but should always be used with the family name in correspondence.

Titles such as *Cavaliere* and *Commendatore* are used alone or followed by the surname (like Signore). (Note: omit the *e* at the end when the title is followed by the surname).

Hereditary titles, such as *Conte, Marchese, Duca*, are followed by the surname and the name of the place.
Correspondence to titled persons should begin with *Egregio* followed by the title and surname. Sign off using "Distinti saluti".

Principal Titles:

> Principe (Principessa)
> Duca (Duchessa)
> Marchese (Marchesa)
> Conte (Contessa)
> Barone (Baronessa)

Chevalier, Ritter, Cavalier etc are also used.

Members of certain families of the nobility – mainly in the South – bear the styles of *Don* and *Donna*. In some families *Donna* is used by all females whilst in others it is not used at all.

The children of a noble without the styles of Don and Donna, and without a territorial title, are addressed, for example as: *Nobile Giacomo dei Conti Attolico*. If with a territorial title: *Nobile Giacomo Attolico dei Conti di Olivero* (dei = of the family).

Jamaica

Mr Enos THOMSON

English forms of address are used except that Mr John Brown may also be addressed in local jargon as *Missa* (Mr). Similarly, Miss Mary Williams may be *Missis* (Miss or Mrs).

Conferred and hereditary titles are used, as in the UK. Thus: Sir Howard Cooke and Lady Cooke. Members of Parliament are addressed as *The Honourable John Brown, Minister of Housing*, etc.

When writing, use the full string of honours. Thus: The Right Honourable Percival Noel James Patterson, MP, PC, Q.C., Prime Minister of Jamaica.

Japan

KITAMURA-san

The family name appears first, followed by the given name. Thus TANAKA Keiko, where Tanaka is the family name, Keiko the given name.

Orally, both men and women are referred to by their family name followed by -san (neutral), -sama (polite ending), -chan (for children, or sometimes affectionately for close friends).

Another suffix freqently used is -*kun*, which is sometimes added to the end of a name when a boss is addressing an underling.

Given names are not used very often, even among long-standing friends and colleagues, except within the family between parents and children, for instance, and perhaps between close friends at university. It is impolite to use the last name of people who are older than you or higher in rank.

For people with rank or position, such as Ministers or Ambassadors, their titles would follow the family name instead of -san. Thus:

Tanaka-koshi = Minister Tanaka.
Kitamura-taishi = Ambassador Kitamura.
Takahashi-shacho = company president Takahashi.

Note that it is customary to address company presidents by their title. These titles usually stand alone when you are addressing those concerned.

These formalities are not appropriate when corresponding by letter unless the correspondence is written in Japanese characters. Therefore for most foreign businessmen such complexities are not relevant. If a letter is written in English, the usual Mr, Mrs, etc. would be used instead of san, sama, etc.

Caution: When speaking or writing English there is a tendency to reverse the order of names.

Japan has abolished the use of titles except for royalty.

Footnote

Never use *san* with your own name when introducing yourself as this effectively means you are honouring yourself.

Traditionally, you will be first introduced to the junior members of a delegation, then the senior members in ascending order of status, though this custom is showing signs of change with increasing exposure to Western businessmen.

Referring correctly to someone's name is viewed as a sign of respect. A business card is studied with gravity, as if it is a resumé. If the name is difficult to pronounce, ask how to say it properly. This will be received as a desire to show respect.

The custom of bowing is multi-purpose as a greeting, an expression of thanks, an apology, a form of respect, and a silent form of address. It is an art form that Westerners are unlikely to get right. One authority illustrates this aptly by reference to a student who bows to his teacher in respect. If years later that student becomes Prime Minister, he would still bow to the teacher. It is a matter of acknowledging one's proper place. Branches of Japanese stores established overseas have tried to transfer the tradition, whereby staff bowed to customers upon entering and leaving the lifts and the store, but found foreigners preferred lower prices instead.

Jordan

Al'Sayid ALI AL-BASHIR

See also the chapter on Arab names.

Mr = *Sayid*   Mrs = *Sayeda*   Miss = *Anesa*

But conversationally you would say, with or without the name:

Al'Sayid   *Al'Sayida*   *Al'Anesa*

Example of a name string:

First Name	Father's name (optional)	Grandfather's name (optional)	Surname
ALI	AHMAD	ZEID	AL-BASHIR

The terms *Abu* and *Um* are used between colleagues, often by those younger to those older, and fall somewhere between using a first name and calling them Mr/Mrs. *Abu* means father of . . . and *Um* is mother of . . . Thus: *Abu Ali* (if Ali is their eldest son), or *Um Ali*.

These terms apply when Ali is the eldest son. If there are no sons, then the eldest daughter. If there is a son, his name will be used instead of the daughters.

The following terms are slightly more familiar in usage:

Al Akh (brother) and *Al Ukhut* (sister) are usually used for those without children. They are also used within a working context. For instance, *Anesa Salwa Kelidar* would be called *Al Ukhut Salwa*, but only if there had been dealings with her before. Otherwise she would be addressed as *Al'Anesa Salwa*.

The parents of friends are referred to as *Ammo* (uncle) or *Khalto* (aunt). As one becomes more mature and has children of one's own, thereby acquiring seniority, these terms are replaced by Um and Abu.

Persons with professional qualifications are addressed as follows:

Engineer:

Al'Muhandis Ali (m)
Al'Muhandisah Laila (f)

Doctor:

Duktor Ali, Duktorah Laila

Kazakhstan

RASHEED Taufikovitch RAHIMBEKOV

There is now a gradual shift away from the traditional use of the patronymic system as used in Russia, though for formal circumstances it is still generally used. This change is a politically sensitive issue. There are also some Turkic influences. About 43% of the population are Kazakhs, 35% Russian, 6% German, 5% Ukrainian, the balance comprising about 100 different ethnic groups.

When adopting Russian honorifics:-

Mr = *Gospodin*   Mrs/Miss = *Gospozha*

However, the use of honorifics is too formal for everyday situations. If using them, you may say Gospodin/Gospozha *firstname*.

There is no distinction between married and unmarried woman.

The forename comes first, then the patronymic which shows filiation to the father, then the surname, which is passed on down the generations.

With the name example above, he is addressed informally as *Rasheed*, omitting the patronymic. More formally he will be *Gospodin Rasheed Taufikovitch*, using the patronymic.

Women change their name upon marriage and surnames may have a feminine form. Thus, Rahimbekov (m); *Rahimbekova* (f).

A polite and informal form of address when younger peopole speak to those who are older is to abbreviate the first name and apply a -*ke* suffix. thus: *Rasheed* will become *Rake*. Similarly, someone named *Bolat* will become *Bake*, and a woman named Umut will become Umuke. Use the forename only.

Recent changes in forms of address largely involve the use of a localised patronymic form. Thus *Rasheed Taufikovitch* becomes *Rasheed-uly*, where *uly* means son of. Similarly, a woman will be addressed as gauhar Rohat-kyzy, where kyzy means daughter of. It is the same for written and oral forms of address.

The Turkic influence is expressed in the use of *-bey* (sir) as a suffix to the forename, as with *Rasheedbey*. This is an informal oral form of address. It is used widely when addressing Kazakh members of the community. There is no feminine equivalent.

In the vernacular:

Mr = *Myrza*   Mrs/Miss = *Bike*

Men who have been to Mecca are addressed (orally and in writing) with *Kajy* after their forename. There is no feminine equivalent.

Kenya

Bwana Amos WAKO

UK forms of address are appropriate for use with the business community and in centres of population.

The dominant language is Swahili. The surname is the last name in the name string, and the honorifics precede the name string or surname.

IN SWAHILI:

Mr = *Bwana*   Mrs/Miss = *Bibi*

It is the same for correspondence. *Binti* is used before the surname by a father to his daughter, or occasionally to address an elderly spinster. Note that when speaking *Bibi* and *Binti* are sometimes abbreviated to *Bi*.

Sometimes *Bi Mchumo* is used for Miss instead of *Binti*, but in Kenya it is considered colloquial (in Tanzania it is not).

Address a doctor of medicine as *Daktari* (then surname). Similarly, address a doctor of philosophy as *Dakta*.

Women usually adopt their husband's surname upon marriage.

Social customs vary according to religion and tribe, of which there are about 45, and name structures sometimes reflect local society. For instance, a person may be named according to the time of birth or the circumstances of the seasons.

Kirghyzia

Myrza IBRAHIMOULOU Asghar
(but see text)

There are many similarities to the forms of address used by Azerbaijan, and we recommend that you refer to that chapter. A patronymic system applies, but traditions have a Turkic base. There are signs of change, but movement towards a Westernised approach is taking hold slowly.

52% of the population is Kirghiz, 22% Russian, 13% Uzbek, and 13% are German, Uighur, Kazakh, and Tajik.

In the vernacular:

Mr = *Myrza*   Mrs = *Aim*   Miss = *Aim*

except that *Kyzym* is preferred to *Aim* when addressing an unmarried woman who is younger than yourself.

In the above name example the ending *oulou* means *son of*. The feminine equivalent is *kyzy* (daughter of).

127

The forename comes first, then the patronymic which shows filiation to the father, then the surname, which is passed on down the generations.

Turning again to the above name example, if addressing him formally, or in an official capacity, say (or write to) *Myrza Ibrahi-moulou*. Informally you may address him as *Myrza Asghar*. The same system applies to the feminine equivalents.

Appendi is the equivalent to the Turkish salutation *Efendi*. In Kirghyzia *Appendi* is used sarcastically, so best avoided.

Kiribati

Mr Peter Timeon

English is spoken and forms of address correspond to those used in the UK except that it is an informal society, so honorifics are generally not used orally. Just use first names.

Korea (North)

JONG Song Gap Tongmu

The family name is first in the name string. With the above example, *Jong* is the family name, *Song* and *Gap* are given names. Most people have three names.

The practice in North Korea differs materially to that in the South (see next chapter).

Ordinary people address one another as *Tongmu* (Comrade), which is gender-neutral and replaces Mr, Mrs, or Miss. It is used either alone or after the last name when speaking or writing to people in the "same category" or class as oneself. Thus: *Jong Song Gap Tongmu*. Alternatively *Tongmu* may be used orally after the family name. Thus: *Jong Tongmu*.

When addressing a "higher person" – someone with position – use *Tongji* instead. *Tongji* is a respect word that is said (or written) after the last name. Thus: *Jong Tongji*.

As a general rule, use *Tongmu* if the person you are addressing is of similar age, but use *Tongji* if they are older. The same applies to men and women.

Close friends use *Tongmu* between themselves, but to distinguish who they are addressing when in company they will use it with the family name.

Women retain their maiden names upon marriage.

Buinnim (Madam) is said alone or after the last name when addressing a Comrade's wife whether at the same level in society or higher. However, when someone clearly higher in status is addressing a woman of lower status the *nim* suffix (which shows respect), is omitted. Thus: *Buin*. (Remember that one may also use the gender-neutral *Tongmu* [Comrade] instead).

Unlike in South Korea, the general name suffix *ssi* is not used, and suffixes such as *nim* are applied differently. The North uses *nim* after the name for teachers and doctors (of any discipline), but does not use it for officials. For instance, a university student would address his teacher like this:

Family name	doctor	teacher	respect word
Kim	Baksa	Sonsaeng	nim

Alternatively, the full name may be used.

There is no distinction between men and women in such forms of address.

A government Minister is addressed orally and in writing as *Buyang Tongji* (Comrade Minister), used either alone or after the name.

Korea (South)

KIM Chul-soo ssi

Korean names begin with the family name, follow with the clan or generation name, and end with the given name. With *Kim Chul-soo* Kim is the family name, Chul is the generation name, and soo is the given name. The generation name is shared by brothers and cousins, and, whenever the family so decides, by one's sisters. It is this name that identifies the origin of the family branch, which reflects on their status within the community. The given name is not a legal name.

Koreans do not use the equivalents of Mr, Mrs, or Miss in Korean, though the use of English honorifics is widely accepted.

There is a hierarchical structure based on Confucian ethics, with people addressed according to their position in society. People are well-nigh never addressed only by their first name, especially within a company.

As a general rule, *ssi* used after the full name with people lower than you in the hierarchy, or among friends. It is not appropriate to use it this way with the elderly. It is also used generally when one is not acquainted with the other but both parties are aware who is the elder of the two. The elder of the two will address the other by name followed by ssi. In the work-place one is usually addressed this way by one's superiors. In extremely formal circumstances, *ssi* is replaced by sonsaengnim (Sir).

There is no special form of address for single women.

Women always retain their maiden name. A married woman will acknowledge a Westerner who addresses her in English as (for instance) *Mrs Kim*, but in Korean she is addressed by her original family name. According to authorities, a Korean husband refers to his wife in various ways, depending on the rank of the person he is speaking to, with the most respectful title being used for introductions to the lowest ranking person. Inexperienced Westerners should not try practising Korean forms of address on a married woman because an over-respectful term might reflect adversely on the status of the husband. A Company President might feel in these circumstances that he is being treated by the Westerner as if he is holding a menial position.

Written and oral forms of address are the same.

However, there are many variables. It is important to show respect, and the appropriate honorifics are contingent upon the situation and the relationship. Age is a also important and betokens degrees of respect. When the boss is the same level as yourself, or if you don't know his position, age may be relevant. Use *ssi* when an elder or someone of higher position addresses a younger person or someone of lower position, but first say the family name.

It is important to use a name with the correct suffix, or you may be considered rude.

Family and friends will use only the given name. Do not address anyone by just the family name, use the full name.

When meeting a businessman for the first time, observe the name card, which will show his position and name. If, for example, he is the supervisor, it will say *Kim Kwajangnim* (Kim the supervisor, where *Kwajang* means *supervisor*). But if you are the supervisor, and he is beneath you in position, omit the *nim* suffix when addressing him. When addressing an executive, his title is always suffixed to his family name, as with Kim Sa-Jang (President Kim), though in English translation it would be prefixed.

As a point of interest, the executive's position is further reflected by the place he takes at table and in his office. For instance, he would sit to the right in the back seat of his car.

There are no special forms of address for professional persons or government officials. The only exception is for doctors (medical and PhDs), who will be addressed like this (male): *Kim Baksa Nim*, where *Kim* is the name, *Baksa* is doctor, and *Nim* is the respect word. A female doctor would be similarly addressed as there is no evident distinction between gender.

The term *Yosa Nim* is used to show respect when addressing an older man or woman than yourself, as with *Kim Yosa Nim*. (The word transcribed as *Yosa* is impossible to represent in English characters, so in this case we recommend that you use English instead).

Caution: The order of people's names is sometimes reversed when Koreans translate them from Korean into romanised text.

Kuwait

Sayed AHMAD Abdulwahab AL-QURTAS

See also the chapter on Arab forms of address.

<blockquote>
Mr = Sayed   Mrs = Sayeda   Miss = Anessa
</blockquote>

There are no hard and fast rules.

Within the string of Arab names everyone usually has their own given name followed by their father's given name. Thus: Mohamad Jemal or Mohamad bin Jemal. Complications arise as the string is added to by the practice of honouring ancestors.

Women also derive their names from their father, and sometimes add their father's father, and so on, ending with their family name. They retain their names after marriage, so they do not take their husband's name.

The use of the full name chain that many Arabs use is for official use on documentation only, for example, for passports and marriage certificates. Otherwise, it is not necessary to refer to all of their names.

In correspondence the rules are again variable. Use their business card as a clue.

Some surnames are derived from tribes as a matter of family policy. The root name (i.e. the last name) is often a description of ancestors, a tribal name, or a place.

Example of the derivation of the name string of a male, Ali Abdullah Mughram Al-Ghamdi:

Given name	Father's name	Grandfather's name	Surname (perhaps tribal name)
Ali	Abdullah	Mughram	Al-Ghamdi

So you will tend always to find a person's given name and always the name of their father, frequently also their grandfather's name, then their tribal-type name, which often, but not always, is preceded by "Al".

The same principle applies to men and to women.

In oral address all that matters will depend entirely on the relationship between the parties.

In general people do not call someone only by their first name except between close social friends. They will always use the honorific before the given name when addressing each other at work. Thus, using the example of the name string above, he would be addressed simply as *Sayed Ali* (Mr Ali).

In correspondence it is usual, but not the rule, to use the honorific followed by the given name, father's name, and last name. Thus: Sayed *Ali Abdullah Al-Ghamdi.* Therefore, if any names are to be left out, they should be those sandwiched between the father's name and the final name in the string.

In our example, the Al-Ghamdi will be carried forward to the next generation, so will always remain the final name in the string.

Titles are very important. Therefore in correspondence address an engineer as: *Engineer Ali Al-Ghamdi.* This also applies to lawyers and doctors. Sometimes it may be stretched to include accountants and architects, but there is no firm rule.

In oral address too, use the full professional title. On subsequent mention one should say simply "Engineer", or "Doctor", etc.

There is often no way to distinguish between a married and an unmarried woman by her names.

There are no firm rules, just probabilities, but when corresponding with a married woman it is customary with many households to do so via the husband.

A single woman whose name, for example, is Taibah Atallah El-Garny would be addressed informally (and orally) by acquaintances as Miss Taibah, but formally as Miss El-Garny. In correspondence she would be addressed as Miss Taibah El-Garny.

The word Sheikh (pronounced like the English word *shake*, with a gurgle on the kh), meaning "old man", is an honorific used among the tribes to describe a tribal leader or man of accepted distinction.

Remember that Kuwait is a Sheikhdom and titles are important. Be sure to use the following tribal honorifics when appropriate (the chapter on Arab names will guide you).

Sheikh (m) Sheikha (f)

Military titles are very important and should always be used.

People with professional qualifications are generally addressed without specific reference to them except for doctors (medical and those with PhDs), and engineers, who will be called, for example, *Engineer Ghazi Al-Rayes*.

Laos

Thao SOMSAVAT Lengsavad

Greet someone with a *wai* (with palms pressed together, as if in prayer), and say *Sabai-dii* (a conventional welcome). We are providing a greeting here exceptionally because it is an important constituent of the ritual involving forms of address.

Mr = *Thao*   Mrs = *Nang*   Miss = *Nangsao*

Sometimes there is no family name. Often, there is only one name. Mr Dang is called *Thao Dang*. Mrs Dang is *Nang Dang*. Miss Dang is *Nangsao Dang*. Where there is more than one name, use the honorific with the first name.

Village peasants are addressed as Thao (m), or Nang (f).

Government officials are addressed as *Thane* (followed by name). A government official's wife is addressed as *Thane Nang*.

Latvia

Jānis SMITA kungs
SMITA kundze

You will need stamina if you want to get this right.

The Russian patronymic system has been abandoned.

Instead of Mr, use *kungs*. For Mrs use *kundze*.
For a very young unmarried woman use *Jaunkundze*.

Do not use *Jaunkundze* except for very young women. Use *kundze*. Indeed, it may be safer to use *kundze* except for children.

It is fairly formal society which uses honorifics *after* the family name, which is the last name in the name string. Moreover, surnames have a genitive ending. Thus Mr Jānis Smits is addressed as *Smita kungs*, his wife is *Smita kundze*.

Don't use first names alone until you have been told to do so.

The present generation is tilting towards informality, but older people will expect you to use *Jūs* (the polite form for "you"). It is customary to use *Jūs* even between colleagues who have been working together for many years.

There are no hereditary or bestowed titles.

In correspondence, use the same formula whereby the family name is followed by the honorific. When writing to husband and wife use, for instance, *Bērziņu ģimenei* to address a letter, where Bērziņu is the surname and ģimenei means "family".

Some people have middle names, which are retained in a person's documents but are usually not used when addressing them.

In correspondence, instead of "Dear", write:-

(To men) Ļoti cienijamais (most respectable) Ļoti godājamais, *or*, augsti godātais (highly honoured).

(To women) Ļoti cienījamā (most respectable) Ļoti godājamā, *or*, augusti godātā (highly honoured), followed by the first name and surname. Thus: Ļoti cienījamā Annai Kalniņas kundzei.

Fortunately, a shortened form is used on envelopes. Ļ. cien / A. god. stands for men and women alike.

When orally addressing an unknown person say: Godātais kungs! / Cienījamā kundze – omitting the names.

Upon marriage, a woman usually adopts her husband's name, but sometimes she will use her maiden name as well, in which case her father's family name precedes her husband's, and is hyphenated.

In postal addresses, the title comes before the position:
Ļoti cienījamam Lauksaimniecības institūta direktoram
Jānim Kalniņa kungam

Address a doctor (of medicine) as doktors / doktoram.
Dr habil. = habilitētais doktors / habilitētajam doktorum
Dr. Hon.c. = goda doktors / goda doktoram.

A person with a degree in science:- Maģ. – maģistrs / maģistram etc.

A director = direktors/-e / direktoram/ei

The oral address for someone with a professional degree does not usually contain the person's name:-

Inženiera (engineer) kungs!   Inženieres kundze!
Arhitekta kungs!   Arhitektes kundze!
Profesora kungs!   Profesores kundze!

Upon familiarity, or to show more respect, you may use the first name or surname with the polite form:

Jāņa kungs!   Annas kundze!

In informal correspondence:

Miļais (Dear) Kalniņa kungs
Miļā Annas kundze

Lebanon

Bassam NAAMANI

The official language is Arabic but there is an important influence from the French language.

It is an informal society and the use of honorifics is not essential. Each community is consistent in that the family name is last. Thus: Joseph HADDAD.

The middle name is usually the father's name, but is frequently omitted. This is a contemporary innovation that has become common practice with all communities.

Women usually take their husband's name upon marriage.

Although French forms of address are usual, you should avoid using the honorific. There are no hard and fast rules, and there are many variations, but in general only first names are used. Such informality applies to Muslim, Christian, and Druze citizens alike. Formerly, it would have been *Monsieur* or *Madame surname*, but not now. Arabs do not use the name string any more.

Exceptionally, Muslims use Anessa for Miss, whilst the other

138

communities would say *Demoiselle* instead. Tribal titles such as *Sheikh* and *Khawaja* are still used.

In the villages Turkish custom tends to encroach, and you would say, for instance, with jocular enthusiasm: *Joseph Efendi*. Many Lebanese use Turkish greetings as oral forms of address only, always in a light-hearted way. This applies to the Druze community too.

Lesotho

Mé Moeketsi TSIBOHO

UK custom is appropriate, especially with the business community. Address people by their family name, which is their last name. Thus Ntsivoa Khabele would be *Mrs Khabele*.

It is local custom to say *Ntate* before the family name when orally addressing any gentleman including one's father. An unmarried woman is addressed as *Ausi* or Mé, and a married woman is addressed as *Mé*.

In correspondence use *Moughali* (Mr) instead of Ntate, and use *Mofumahatsana* for an unmarried woman.

Hereditary titles, denoting tribal lines of descent, are signified by the use of:

Motlotlehi	King
Mufumahali	Queen
Khosi	Prince
Khosatsana	Chieftainess / Princess
Morena	Chief (masc). NB: When the Chief's wife is standing in for the Chief, she is then addressed as Morena.

The above titles are used before the forename and surname.

Mosali (pronounced Mosadi) and *Monna* are conferred titles, which become *Mé* and *Ntate* in written form. These are used before the family name.

Persons of rank are addressed, both orally and in writing, as *Mohiomphehi*.

Someone with a professional degree, such as an engineer, is addressed as *Ngaka*. Persons of learning are *Tichere* (teacher), and doctors are *Doktor*. These may be used with or without the name.

Liberia

Mr George Bardell COOPER

UK forms of address are used.

Married women adopt their husband's family name.

There are no hereditary or conferred titles except within the tribes. It is not necessary to know the many tribal customs for general business purposes.

Libya

See also the chapter on Arab names.

Name strings are very much like those of the Gulf and there are no hard and fast rules. Everything is loose and variable. However, Libya is a revolutionary country and conventional honorifics have been generally swept away.

Libya is traditionally a tribal and clan society, but the honorific *Sheikh* is not used.

Address people as Al-Akh (brother) or El-Oaht (sister), followed (usually, but not always) by the first name of their name string. Thus: *Al-Akh Mohammed* and *El-Oaht Selma Rashid*. (There is no precise transliteration of the *kh*-sound in English. It is similar to the *ch* in Scots *loch*).

In the following example of a name string that we have used for other Arab countries, the structure for Libya would be similar, with many (but not all) families having the *Al* prefix, indicating a tribe. He would be addressed as *Al-Ch Ali*.

Given name	Father's name	Grandfather's name	Surname, perhaps tribal name
Ali	Abdullah	Mughram	Al-Ghamdi

Persons with professional qualifications are addressed as such. An engineer is Al Mohandess; a doctor is Al Doctor; and a lawyer is Al Muhami.

Liechtenstein

Herr Paul KINDLE

German is spoken and forms of address correspond to those used in Germany.

Mr = *Herr*   Mrs = *Frau*

Women up to the age of about 18 are addressed as Fräulein, but are thereafter often addressed as Frau.

Refer to the chapter on Germany for more details.

Lithuania

Ponas Vincas BALICKAS

The use of English is acceptable for both oral and written communication, and is used in exactly the same way as for the United Kingdom.

In the vernacular

Mr = *Ponas*   Mrs = *Ponia*   Miss = *Panelé*

Use these either alone (like *Sir*, or *Madam*), or with the family name.

Luxembourg

Här Constance MOLITOR

Luxembourg follows French practice for correspondence, but uses an original form of oral address.

The given name is followed by the family name.

For oral conversation, use *with* the family name:

Mr = *Här*   Mrs = *Madame*   Miss = *Joffer*

For written communication use: Monsieur, Madame, or Mademoiselle, as appropriate. Sign off letters: "Veuillez agréer Monsieur, l'expression de mes sentiments les meilleurs." (equivalent to Yours faithfully).

Titles are no longer conferred.

Order of family names for people with hereditary titles:

Grand Duc Jean de Luxembourg
Baron (family name)
Comte de (geographical name, such as: *Vianden*)

For persons of rank (Oral):

Här Minister
Här Colonel
Här Ambassadeur

In writing:

Monsieur le Ministre
Mon Colonel
Monsieur l'Ambassadeur

To orally address persons with professional degrees:

Här Ingénieur (engineer)
Här Dokter (doctor)

But when writing, use:

Monsieur l'ingénieur
Monsieur le docteur

Macao

Mrs GU Jingxian

Most citizens are of Chinese origin, and the forms of address described in the Hong Kong chapter will be appropriate.

Therefore the first name is the family name and the next name(s) is the given name. Say Mr/Mrs *first name*.

Those who are Portuguese are in the minority, and they are addressed as described in the Portugal chapter:

Mr = *Senhor*   Miss / Mrs = *Senhora*

Unmarried women are also addressed as Minha Senhora.

Macedonia

Gospodin Dimce NIKOLOV

Mr = *Gospodin*   Mrs = *Gospogja*   Miss = *Gospogjica*

Although family names have masculine and feminine endings, forms of address conform to Western custom, and you address people as Mr / Mrs last-name (family name). Thus: *Gospodin Nikolov.*

His wife would be *Gospogja Nikolova.*

Family names that end with *ov* for men will therefore convert to *ova* for women.

Informally, whether writing or speaking, use just the first name, as with *Dimce.*

Madagascar

Monsieur Benjamin RAKOTOFAMOLA

Use French forms of address (see chapter on France).

Mr = *Monsieur*   Mrs = *Madame*   Miss = *Mademoiselle*

Most married women adopt their husband's family name upon marriage, though many don't.

Unlike France, there are neither bestowed nor hereditary titles.

Malawi

Mr Tony KANDIERO

English and Chichewa are the official languages, though many dialects are spoken.

The use of English is acceptable for both oral and written communication, in exactly the same way as for the United Kingdom.

Malaysia

Encik Mohamad NOOR bin Mat Isa

There are no family names. A man is known by his given name(s) followed by bin (son of) followed by his father's name.

When a man has two given names he is usually, but not always, addressed by using the second, e.g. *Mohamed Khir bin Johari* would be known as *Khir Johari*. The "bin" is often dropped.

A Malay woman is known by her given name(s) followed by binte (daughter of) followed by her father's name.

All ethnically Malay names are Muslim names.

bin / ibni	Son of
binte	Daughter of
Encik (pronounced I*nchek*)	Mr
Puan	Mrs
Cik (pronounced *Chek*)	Miss

Haji	Used before a man's name to indicate that he has performed the Haj.
Tuan	Honorific used before Haji if person has no higher title.

Tuan is a title of respect for older and distinguished people. Puan is the female equivalent.

Conferred titles

Tun	Highest federal award to a commoner.
Toh Puan	Wife of a Tun.
Tan Sri	Second most senior federal award for commoners.
Puan Sri	Wife of a Tan Sri.
Dato' / Datuk	third most senior award for commoners.
Datin	Wife of a Dato' or Datuk. Not used for husbands of female Datuks in their own right.
Datuk Seri	High grade Datukship.

Some hereditary titles

Tengu / Tunku (both pronounced *Tun-koo*)	Prince or Princess.
Raja	denotes person of Royal descent.

Indian Names

Indian women take their husband's family name upon marriage. *Hindu Indians* incorporate their father's first names rather than family names. Please refer to the chapter on Singapore for further details but note that in Malaysia most Indians, including Sikhs, have A/L or A/P inserted before the family name on official documents (such as identity passes). This stands for *Anak Lelaki* (son of) and

Anak Perembuan (daughter of) respectively. Thus: *Joseph A/L Sin-naveriah*. Most married Indian women retain this style on their official documents throughout their lifetime. *A/L* and *A/P* are not used in oral forms of address and are optional for written forms.

Chinese Names

Chinese surnames precede Chinese given names. For example, with Liew Sip Hon – Liew is the surname and Sip Hon the given name (used together). Some Chinese also embrace English forenames, thus Michael Chen Wing Sum may be known as Michael Chen or as Chen Wing Sum.

See also the note on dialects under China.

Portuguese Names

There is also a small community of Catholic Eurasians, of Portuguese descent, located near Malacca. They speak Kristang, an archaic dialect once spoken in Portugal, and retain Portuguese family names. They will also speak Malay and for practical purposes it is unnecessary to know Kristang forms of address.

Maldives

People have Arab names except that the name string is usually shortened, with most people having just two names, though some have three.

In the vernacular (Dhivehi) use:

Mr = *Alfarlil*   Miss & Mrs = *Arfarlilla*

For practical purposes, English forms of address should be acceptable, so you may distinguish unmarried women by addressing them as Miss. In contrast to nearby Sri Lanka, for formal occasions use the honorific with the first name or with both names (if the subject has two). Informally, just use the second name, though it is also acceptable to use just the first name.

Mali

Monsieur Demba MACALOU

Mr = *Monsieur*   Mrs = *Madame*   Miss = *Mademoiselle*

The use of French forms of address is acceptable (See chapter on France).

Address a company director as *Monsieur le directeur*, and a government Minister as *Monsieur le ministre*.

Malta

Mr Walter SULTANA

Use UK custom for forms of address in ordinary situations. Exceptions are described below.

Medical doctors, lawyers, and people with PhDs are all addressed as Dr.

Architects are just *Mr*, but in correspondence engineers are *Mr* with their degree at the end of the name.

MPs and Ministers are addressed as *Honourable*. Ambassadors are *Excellency*.

Malta bestows hereditary and conferred titles, and when a person has a title, it is used. The son of someone with a hereditary title is also entitled to a specific form of address.

Chevalier (a knight of Malta) is a conferred title awarded to men, but the son is Mr. There is no special title for the spouse.

In correspondence use: *Chev.*
Orally, address him as *Chevalie*.

Maltese titles are *Marquis (m)*, *Marquesa (f)*, *Count (m)*, *Countessa (f)*, *Baron (m)*, and *Baronessa (f)*. The head of the family in each case is addressed as The Most Noble (then title). Address the heir as *Marchesino*, *Contino*, or *Baroncino* respectively.

Other sons and daughters are addressed as *The Noble* (then forename and title).

Marshall Islands

Marshallese and English are the official languages. Use American English forms of address.

Martinique

Use French forms of address. Refer to the chapter on France for further details.

Mr = *Monsieur*   Mrs = *Madame*   Miss = *Mademoiselle*

Mauritania

Monsieur Ahmed ould Ghanahallah

The official languages are French and Hassaniya Arabic (an Arabic dialect). The administrative language is French.

There are no rules governing which name of a person's name string to address formally. It might be any of them. It is best to ask.

There is some similarity in name structure to that of Gulf Arabia, with *ould* often inserted by men between their names, meaning *son of*. Similarly, women insert *ment* between their names, meaning "daughter of", as with *Moulkhair ment Mattalee*. With Arab names in the Gulf there are sometimes clues as to how to address someone (see chapter on Arab forms of address), but with Mauritania there are none. For instance, Ahmed Sidi El Mehdi may be addressed as *Ahmed* between friends, or as *Monsieur El Mehdi* formally. On the other hand, it might be any combination or sequence – there is no rule.

Women retain their maiden names upon marriage.

Mauritius

Mr (or Messieurs) Mohundass DULLOO

Creole is spoken but English is the official language and forms of address may be used in the same way as they are used in the UK, especially for correspondence.

When using Creole, which is an oral patois, say:

Mr = *Messieurs*   Mrs = *Madam*   Miss = *Mamselle*

Place the honorific before the surname (last name).

Mexico

Señor Juan GÓMEZ Sánchez

SPANISH IS SPOKEN.

See also the chapter on Spanish American forms of address.

Mr = *Señor*   Mrs = *Señora*   Miss = *Señorita*

The given name is followed by the father's surname, then the mother's surname. Thus: *Juan Gómez Sánchez.*

For oral address, follow the honorific with the father's surname. Address him as *Señor Gómez.*

When writing, use the full name string. Thus: *Señor Juan Gómez Sánchez.*

In writing, married women use *Señora* followed by the given name, father's surname, de (of), then the husband's surname. Thus: *Señora María García de Gómez*. Orally, one would normally address and refer to a married woman by her preferred surname, e.g. *Señora Campora* or *Señora de Campora*. For verbal communication, *Señora Díaz de Campora* is too long. The same applies to unmarried women. *Srta. María García* is too long, so one would tend to say *Srta. García* in conversation.

Bárbara Gómez Sánchez, an unmarried woman, would be addressed as *Señorita Gómez*.

When informality is appropriate, use the given name. Thus: *Juan*, *María*, or *Bárbara*.

Note that in Mexico any woman who is not familiar to you is addressed as Señorita, whether she is a waitress, hotel receptionist, telephone operator, or whatever. You may feel uncomfortable addressing a woman of 90 as Señorita, but it is correct.

There are no hereditary titles.

Professional titles:

An engineer = Ingeniero (Ing. in correspondence) – as with Ing. Juan Gómez Sánchez.
An accountant = C.P. But, if the accountant has a degree (they usually do), use Licenciado orally.
Doctor = Dr. for men, and Dra. for women.

A person with a degree other than the above is a Licenciado, abbreviated in correspondence to Lic., as with *Lic. Juan Gómez Sánchez* or *Lic. María Gómez Sánchez*.

When writing one has the option as to whether or not to place the honorific before the courtesy title, as with: Sr. Lic. Gómez. Generally omit the honorific unless you prefer to be formal. Do not use the honorific when speaking, just the courtesy title, thus: Licenciado Gómez.

Such forms of address as *Don* and *Doña*, which are used for persons of standing by many Spanish-speaking countries in Latin America, tend to be less frequently used in Mexico. However, they are often used in the provinces, especially for formal occasions, such as weddings. Otherwise, use them only, for example, for diplomatic and very formal occasions. Do not place the honorific beforehand.

Example: *Don Carlos; Doña María.*

Su Excelencia would be an appropriate form of address to persons of standing in the community, such as Ministers.

Micronesia

Mr Aloysius TUUTH

Forms of address correspond to those used in the USA.

Moldova

Domnule Chiric MIHAI Ion

Forms of address correspond to those used in Russia although the Moldovan language is a derivative of Romanian. Therefore use Romanian honorifics, with the Russian patronymic system

When speaking to Mr Marin, he should be addressed as "Domnule Marin" (first name, Gheorghe, is not mentioned.)

When writing to Mr Marin, he should be addressed as "Domnul Gheorghe Marin" (no "e" after "Domnul"), or "Dl. Gheorghe Marin" (in the address), and at the beginning of the letter as

"Stimate domn" ("Dear Sir"). Similarly, Mrs and Miss at the beginning of a letter should be "Stimată doamnă" and "Stimată domnişoară".

Oral forms of address:

> Mr = *Domnule*   Mrs = *Doamnă*   Miss = *Domnişoară*
>   (when addressing a person unknown to the speaker)

or

> Mr = *Domnule*   Mrs = *Doamna*   Miss = *Domnisoara*
>   (when followed by the person's surname (e.g. Domnule Marin)

The following terms are used in correspondence (in the address only):

> Mr = *Domnul*   Mrs = *Doamna*   Miss = *Domnişoara*

Abbreviations used in correspondence (in the address only):

> Mr = *Dl.*   Mrs = *D-na*   Miss = *D-ra*

Since Moldova became independent of Russia there has been an inclination to arrest the use of the third name in the name string. So, in the above example, Ion would tend not to be used, though it remains in existence.

With Russian-type names, the forename comes first, then the patronymic which shows filiation to the father, then the surname, which is passed on down the generations. Thus: Ivan Ivanovitch Tolstoy (m) would be addressed as *Ivan Ivanovitch*. If we refer to Tatiana Ivanovna (f), Ivanovna is the feminine patronymic of Ivan and is therefore the daughter.

See the chapter on Russia for further details.

Monaco

Monsieur Jacques Louis BOISSON

Mr = *Monsieur*   Mrs = *Madame*   Miss = *Mademoiselle*

Forms of address correspond entirely to those used in France except that the Principality has a Royal family and all entitled members are addressed as follows:

Orally: *Monseigneur*

Orally and for correspondence: *Votre Altessa Serenissime (Your Serene Highness.*

These are the same whether masculine or feminine. Do not use the above with the name. In the third person you would, for instance, speak of Prince Rainier.

Mongolia

Mr Dashiin BOLD

The first part of the first name is derived from the father's name and the second name is the given name. Thus: With *Dashiin Bold*, "Dash" derives from the father. An alternative to the suffix iin on the father's name is yn. People are addressed by the honorific with the given name. Thus: *Mr Bold*. Similarly, Tsenendorjiin Jambaldorj is *Mr Jambaldorj*, although it is his given name.

As stated, in conversatioin *Dashiin Bold* would be called *Mr Bold*. Do not say both names. When writing, it is customary to use capitals for the given name. Thus: on the envelope: Mr BOLD, or Mr D. BOLD.

Nowadays many Mongolians omit the ending (*iin* or *yn*) in correspondence. Thus, at the head of your letter you may write *Dash BOLD* (where BOLD is the given name), but open (as stated): Dear Mr BOLD.

The same also applies to married and unmarried women. Women do not change their name upon marriage.

With some names, such as *Choisurengiin*, the *g* has been added because the suffix is *iin*, but it is omitted when the suffix is *yn*. The name (as distinct from the person) has gender. A man can have a male name with a feminine ending, and vice versa.

Transliteration of Mongolian into English is difficult, but in general the use of the letters a,o,y and a,o,u in a name indicates that it is masculine and that the suffix *yn* is appropriate. The use of e,i,u and e,u,y in a name suggests it is feminine, and the suffix *iin* is appropriate instead.

There are neither hereditary titles nor any special forms of address for persons with professional degrees (such as engineers), though you should always use the usual professional titles (doctor, professor, etc) when appropriate. Use them with the given name (last name).

Morocco

Sayed BENNIS Abdel-Ilah

The official language is Arabic but French is widely used.

Mr = *Sayed*   Miss / Mrs = *Lalla*

Family names exist and usually appear first in the name string. The name string ordinarily comprises just two names, which, unlike the Gulf coutnries, are not connected by the use of *bin* or *al* (son of). The exception is when the Prophet's name is given to males, which will appear first (as Mohammad) in the string but is rarely mentioned when addressing someone.

Hyphenated names, as with *Abdel-Ilah* in the above example, are held to be one name.

Therefore use the honorific before the family name: *Sayed Bennis*.

However, *Sayed* may be abbreviated to *Si*, and is used in this form before either the family name, or, with more familiarity, before the given names. Thus: *Si Bennis*, or *Si Abdel-Ilah*.

Women use *Lalla* before the given name, not the family name.

Always use the honorific until familiarity is sufficiently obvious for the use of the given names to be mutually acceptable. This will not take long to achieve.

A man or boy known to be a *Shorfa* (member of a family descending from the Prophet) is entitled to be addressed as Moulay. The woman or girl is addressed as Lalla. Whether orally or in correspondence these titles are used before the given name.

Women usually retain their maiden names after marriage. Official documents, such as passports, give their names, followed by the entry *spouse of . . .*

There are no particular forms of address for persons with professions.

Spanish and English are also widely understood, though French forms of address are the natural alternative to Arabic.

Use:

Monsieur   Madame   Mademoiselle

Oral and written forms are the same except that instead of Mademoiselle use the abbreviation *Melle*.

In correspondence the family name appears first, followed by given name(s). Thus: *Monsieur Hamdan Hassan*, where Hamdan is the family name. Similarly, it will be *Madame Hamdan* and *Melle. Hamdan* (Miss).

formal invitations are addressed to Monsieur/Madame *Family Name* then *Given Name*.

However, the order is reversed for oral communication. A business-man meeting someone for the first time would use both names, then say Monsieur HASSAN on subsequent meetings. Colleagues tend to say both names (given name then family name). Government officials, for instance, always address one another by their given name then family name.

References to someone in the third person are by saying the given name then family name.

Mozambique

Senhor Emílio Zefanias MUCAVLE

Portuguese is spoken by all classes, with English spoken in business circles.

Citizens are referred to orally as *Senhor* (Mr) or *Senhora* (Mrs).

Forms of address correspond largely to those used in Portugal, but people are addressed formally by only the last name in the name string. Less formally, sometimes men and woman are addressed by their first name, as with *Senhor Emílio*.

When informality is appropriate address people usually by their first given name (sometimes they will opt for their second given name), without the honorific, thus: *Emílio*.

Unmarried women are generally addressed orally and in writing as *Mnina*.

Sometimes *Dona* is preferred to Senhora in speech or correspondence, as with: *Dona Marta Baptista de Paula*, and is apt for addressing what are described as "respectable married women". Call her *Dona Marta*, but write to the name in full or the initials and *de Paula*.

Men usually place their mother's maiden name before the father's surname. A married woman may retain her maiden surname before her married surname.

The visitor may occasionally be addressed as Camarada (comrade), but this is not correct outside FRELIMO party circles, and is discouraged. Ao Senhor is the more usual written form of address to men; the feminine equivalent is À Sra. Orally, omit the Ao or À.

In correspondence use all names, even when there is a long name string.

There are no conferred or hereditary titles, but professional people are addressed accordingly. Address a professor as *Senhor Professor* (abbreviate to Prof. for ordinary schoolteachers).

Address a doctor as *Senhor Doutor* (m) or Senhora Doutora (f) (do not abbreviate), an engineer as *Senhor Engenheiro* or Senhora Engenheira, an architect as *Senhor Arquitecto* or *Senhora Arquitecta*. The university and degree should be placed after the name. In correspondence, write, for instance: *Exmo. Senhor Dr.*, or: *Exmo. Senhor Arqto.* etc, followed by the full name.

Those with degrees of Licenciado or Bacharel are styled Dr. (*Doutor* is only written in full for anyone with a doctor's degree).

A Minister is addressed orally as *Senhor Ministro / Senhora Ministra*. Similarly, an Ambassador is *Senhor Embaixador/Senhora Embaixadora*. In correspondence, write *Sua Excelência*, followed by rank.

His/her excellency = *Sua Excelencia*
Distinguished gentlemen = *Exmo Sr.*
Your excellency = *Excelencia*

Namibia

Mr Albertus Madawa NARUSEB

Namibia is a multicultural society with more than eleven vernaculars spoken. It is therefore impractical to provide a useful selection of the different forms of address for all of them.

For the purposes of general communication, Namibians have adopted English as the lingua franca, and in this context oral forms of address for ordinary citizens accord to the usual Mr Mrs and Miss format.

People of both sexes are known by their family name. Thus: Josia James would be addressed as *Mr James*.

First names are used informally only between people who know one another well.

Nauru

Mr Vinci CLODUMAR

Forms of address correspond to those used in the UK.

There is some formality, especially when addressing senior politicians and eminent people. All government Ministers are addressed in correspondence as *The Honourable* (plus both names) followed by the initials *MP*. (Member of Parliament). Orally, in the third person or for introduction, say *The Honourable* (add names).

When speaking to an MP address him or her as *Minister*.

The President of Nauru is addressed orally as Your Excellency, and in correspondence as *His Excellency The Honourable Bernard Dowiyogo, MP*.

Nepal

Mr Chandra Bahadur MAHARJAN

Forms of address in Nepal correspond largely to those used in the UK.

There is a royal family which is addressed in the same way that the British royal family is addressed.

Netherlands

De Heer Joop HOEKMAN

The Dutch system is very complex and full details are not necessary because English is acceptable.

In Dutch, Mr = Mijnheer, but is regarded as old fashioned and somewhat "correct". It is now largely superseded by *De Heer*.

Mr = *De Heer*   Mrs = *Mevrouw*   Miss = *Mejuffrouw*

To a woman over a loosely defined 21–30, always use Mrs/Mevrouw. The equivalent to *Ms* is *Mw*.

Persons with professional qualifications are given the title before the initials and instead of Mr/Mrs. So *Ir.* (the abbreviation for correspondence to an "insinjur" – engineer), is the correct form of address for a graduate of engineering. Thus: *Ir. Hoekman*. (Note: *Ir.* is equivalent to a BSc and is used for someone who has obtained a degree at a technical college. For someone who has achieved a degree at university, use *Ing.* instead.)

Remember to place the qualification before the name.

Drs. applies to a male graduate generally (but not engineering or law). *Dra* is the female equivalent.
A male graduate in economics is addressed as *Dr.* and a woman as *Drs.*
A law graduate is *Mr.*
A male graduate in letters is *Dr.* and a woman is *Drs.*

As people with professional degrees retain the use of their letters in formal correspondence, when writing, address De Heer Joop HOEKMAN, a person with a degree, as:

Ir. Joop Hoekman when he is an engineer.
Prof. Drs. Ir. Hoekman when he is a Professor of Engineering.
Drs. Hoekman M.Sc. when he has a doctorate in another science.
SH Joop Koekman when he is a lawyer.

It is not customary to address people by their forenames, though this is beginning to change.

There are 4 hereditary titles, with accompanying titles for wives: graaf (m) and gravin (f); Baron (m) and Barones (f); Ridder; and Jonkheer (m) and Mevrouw (f), but Dutch titles are not used in speech and everyone may be addressed as Mr Mrs or Miss.

In correspondence to those entitled (but not in speech), *Freule* is the title for an unmarried lady of nobility.

The unmarried daughter of a Jonkheer is a Jonkvrouwe.

Conferred honours are referrred to neither in speech nor in correspondence.

Netherlands Antilles
(including Curaçao, Bonaire, Saba,
St Eustatius, St Maarten, and Aruba)

Dutch is the official language recognised by Parliament. Papiemento (derived from Dutch, Spanish, and Portuguese) is usually spoken on Curaçao, Bonaire, and Aruba. English is also widely spoken. Aruba is an autonomous nation.

Most citizens have been schooled in Dutch, and Dutch forms of address are those that are commonly used.

Mr = *De Heer*   Mrs = *Mevrouw*   Miss = *Mejuffrouw*

For more information please refer to the chapter on the Netherlands.

Note that South St Maarten belongs to the Netherlands Antilles, but the North (known as St Martin) is French, being part of the French Antilles (West Indies) and French forms of address are used there:

Mr = *Monsieur*   Mrs = *Madame*   Miss = *Mademoiselle*

New Caledonia

French is spoken and forms of address correspond to those used in France.

Mr = *Monsieur*   Mrs = *Madame*   Miss = *Mademoiselle*

New Zealand

Mr George F. GAIR

Forms of address in New Zealand correspond to those used in the UK, though "Ms" is more commonplace, with unmarried women usually adopting it.

Conferred and hereditary titles apply to those entitled, and UK forms of address are appropriate.

Nicaragua

Señor Carlos DOMÍNGUEZ Vargas

SPANISH IS SPOKEN.

See also the general chapter on Spanish American forms of address.

Mr = *Señor*   Mrs = *Señora*   Miss = *Señorita*

In correspondence:

Sr.   Sra.   Srta.

The given name is usually followed by the father's family name, then the mother's family name. Spanish forms of address apply with all communities, but name structures are not always in the traditional Spanish American format, though the majority are.

Address a man by his father's name. Thus: Señor Carlos Domínguez Vargas will be called *Señor Domínguez*, but write to him using all names.

Married women use *Señora* followed by the given name, father's surname, *de* (of), then husband's surname, as described in the chapter on Spanish-American forms of address. If there is uncertainty as to whether or not a woman is married, you should say *Señorita* followed by her given name and father's name. Remember that a young unmarried woman would be addressed as *Señorita*; a more mature woman would be addressed as *Señora* whether married or not.

Use the full name string in correspondence.

Matters become complicated because many people have de as a

normal component of their name structure, so it does not always indicate marriage in a woman's name.

If writing to the husband and wife together, when the wife is not using her husband's family name address them like this: *Señor Carlos Domínguez Vargas and Señora María García Garde.*

There are no hereditary titles.

The courtesy titles *Don* and *Doña* are used for eminent persons. Say: *Señor Don* (m) or *Señora Doña* (f) followed by the given name. Thus: *Señor Don Carlos* and *Señora Doña María.*

Indeed, *Don and Doña may also be used politely instead of Señor /a* for people in ordinary society, but do not use *Señor /a* beforehand.

There are no hereditary or conferred titles.

Professional titles: Someone with a degree in engineering is written to as *Señor/a Ingeniero/Ingeniera*, and someone with a university degree in any subject is a *Licenciado* (Thus: Senhor/a Lic.)
In correspondence use *Ing., Lic., Dr.,* respectively, but begin with the professional title followed by the given name, then the father's surname, then the mother's surname. Thus: *Dr. Orlando Morales García.*

In oral address use the honorific followed by the father's surname (Thus: *Señor Domínguez*). Do not refer to the person's professional title.

A medical doctor or person with a doctorate in any discipline is a *Doctor* (m) or *Doctora* (f) and is addressed as such in writing or speech.

A Minister is addressed orally as *Señor Ministro* (Minister). An ambassador is *Señor Embajador*. When writing, begin with the complete name and rank. Thus: *Dr. Orlando Morales Garcia, Ministro de Turismo.*

Niger

Monsieur Bawa BAKO

Mr = *Monsieur*   Mrs = *Madame*   Miss = *Mademoiselle*

French is used exclusively for official and commercial purposes. Use the usual French forms of address.

Nigeria

Mr Yaswat Dahi GUKAS

Forms of address in Nigeria correspond sufficiently to those used in the UK, where the family name is the last name of the name string. Thus: Mr William KEFAS.

There are many tribal languages, with the Yoruba, Hausa, and Ibo tribes representing the three principal languages, but it is not necessary to know their forms of address. English honorifics are widely acceptable.

Male Muslims who have been to Mecca prefix their name with *Alhaji*, which replaces the honorific (do not say Mr Alhaji. . .).

When writing to a prominent personality, place his/her title below the name. Do not refer to the title in oral forms of address. Thus:

His Excellency Alhaji Abubaker Alhaji,
Sardauna of Sokoto (traditional ruler of Sokoto).

A woman who has visited Mecca precedes her name with *Hajia*, (omitting *Al*).

Women take their husband's family name upon marriage.

Tribal Chiefs should always be addressed by their title. Thus: *Chief Emeka Anyaoku*, who may be addressed orally and for the opening of correspondence as *Chief Anyaoku*.

Engineers and doctors are usually addressed as such, but this is not as important for those in other professions.

Norway

(Mr) Kjeli ELIASSEN

A very informal society where honorifics are generally not used. Use the first name with the family name (last name). Thus Viggo Smestad is addressed without formality as *Viggo Smestad* (without the Mr).

Never say "Mrs."

In speech, one seldom uses names, just saying "good morning", or whatever. If, on the other hand, you refer to someone in the third person at a business meeting, use both his/her names or at least refer to his/her family name.

Business letters are just as informal – omit the honorifics. Start your letter with a subject heading, but do not start with "Dear". This will seem strange to those unfamiliar with Norwegian practice, but it is correct, though a business letter from a foreigner writing in English will be excused if it starts with *Dear Mr Surname*. In English, sign off in the usual way. In Norway the equivalent of "Dear", followed by the first name, is used in correspondence only between friends.

However, professional qualifications are often used in correspondence, so address someone as *Engineer Smestad*, or *Lawyer Smestad*, etc. Do not be so formal with oral forms of address.

Upon marriage some women keep their maiden name only, some add their husband's family name to their maiden name, and others use the husband's name only.

There are no titles.

Oman

Sayed ABDULLAH bin Mohamed Al Dhahab

See also the chapter on Arab forms of address.

The general practice is to use *Sayed* (Mr) or *Sayeda* (Mrs) with the first name only. Thus: Abdullah bin Mohamed Al Dhahab will be addressed as *Sayed Abdullah*. This applies to both oral and written forms of address.

There are no hard and fast rules with Arab names. Everything is loose and variable, and different influences will govern the practices of each Arab country.

Within the string of Arab names everyone usually has their own given name followed by their father's given name. Thus: Mohamad Jemal or Mohamad bin Jemal. Complications arise as the string is added to by the practice of honouring ancestors.

Women also derive their names from their father, and sometimes add their father's father, and so on, ending with their family name. They retain their names after marriage, and do not take their husband's name.

The full name chain that many Arabs use is for official use on documentation only, for example for passports and marriage certificates. Otherwise, it is not necessary to refer to them all.

In correspondence the rules are again variable. Use business cards as a clue.

Some surnames are derived from tribes as a matter of family policy. The root name (i.e. the last name) is often a description of ancestors, a tribal name, or a place.

Example of the derivation of the name string of a male, Ali Abdullah Mughram Al-Ghamdi:

Given name	Father's name	Grandfather's name	Surname, perhaps tribal name
Ali	Abdullah	Mughram	Al-Ghamdi

People do not generally call someone only by their first names except between close social friends. They will always use the honorific before the given name when addressing each other at work. Thus, using the example of the name string above, he would be addressed simply as Sayed Ali.

In the Gulf States "Al" indicates "tribe of".

In *correspondence* it is usual, but not the rule, to use the honorific followed by the given name, father's name, and last name. Thus: *Sayed Ali Abdullah Al-Ghamdi*. Therefore, if any names are to be left out, they should be those sandwiched between the father's name and the final name in the string.

Titles are very important. Therefore in correspondence address an engineer as: *Engineer Ali Al-Ghamdi*. This also applies to lawyers and doctors. Sometimes it may be stretched to include accountants and architects, but there is no firm rule.

In oral address too, use the full professional title. On subsequent mention one should say simply "Engineer", or "Doctor", etc.

There is often no way to distinguish between a married and an unmarried woman by their names.

When corresponding to a married woman it is customary with many households to do so via the husband. Different Arab countries apply different formulas to this and use different customs to distinguish the provenance of the female by the names.

A single female whose name is Taibah Atallah El-Garny would be addressed informally (and orally) by acquaintances as *Miss Taibah*, but formally as *Miss El-Garny*.

In correspondence she would be addressed as *Miss Taibah El-Garny*.

Titles

Individual Arab countries tend to employ distinct titles for members of royal families. Amir and Sultan are the preferred Royal titles, there is also Effendi (Turkish derivative), and Imam (religious teacher). Sheikh is tribal. Military titles are very important and should always be used.

The word Sheikh, meaning "old man", is an honorific used among the tribes to describe a tribal leader or man of widely accepted distinction.

In the Sultanate of Oman members of the royal family are addressed as Amir (Prince) and Amira (Princess). The head of the royal family is the Sultan.

Pakistan

Janab Mian Riaz SAMEE

Forms of address in Pakistan correspond largely to those of the UK for the educated and business communities.

However, it is useful to know the following:

Say Begum (Madam) when referring to a married woman, or when introducing your own wife, but say Begum Sahiba when *addressing* a married woman. You may also use Sahiba after the operative name (see below).

Miss = *Ansa*, but is seldom used. English "Miss" is more appropriate.

It is not common to use *Mr* before a name, even in business circles. Use it only when you intend to maintain distance. Instead, use Sahib after the operative part of the name, though there is now a trend away from this and towards *Mr* in some circles.

The *operative* part of the name may be difficult to determine. Some people prefer to use their first name, others use their family name. If in doubt, ask. Remember that there is no established system for family names, nor is the familiar Muslim custom of having "son of" applied in Pakistan.

For example, with Abdul Hafiz Mirza, Mirza is a clan name that has been added later. He may be addressed either as *Mirza Sahib*, or as *Hafiz Sahib*.

Women usually take their husbands family name on marriage, though their names may be in any order.

Family or clan names are used, such as:
Choushry, Mian, Malik, Raja, etc.

Janab(m) is used before a person's name when addressing bosses, elders, or peers. Do not use it for close friends or with those with whom you are on first name terms. The female equivalent is Mohtaima, as with *Mohtaima Benazir Bhutto*. Or, you could say *Benazir Bhutto Sahiba*.

To show respect, doctors and lawyers are addressed as *Doctor Sahib* and *Wakil Sahib* respectively.

Some conferred titles are: *Mir*, *Nawab*, and *Sardar*. Sardar is a title of a tribal chief, though there are also people who have Sardar as a name.

Palau (Belau)

Mr Tommy REMENGESAU

English and Palauan are the official languages. Use American English forms of address.

Panamá

Señor *Licenciado* José ANTONIO Burgos

SPANISH IS SPOKEN.

See also the chapter on Spanish American forms of address.

Mr = *Señor*   Mrs = *Señora*   Miss = *Señorita*

In correspondence abbreviate to:

Sr.   Sra.   Srta.

The given name is followed by the father's surname, then the mother's surname.

Using this example of a name string: Señora Alba DOMÍNGUEZ de Farhat, address her by her father's family name. Thus: *Señora Domínguez*.

In conversation, married women use *Señora* followed by the given name and father's surname. In correspondence add de (of) between the father's surname and husband's surname.

A young unmarried woman would be addressed as *Señorita*. A more mature woman would be addressed as *Señora* whether married or not. When a woman's status is in doubt, call her *Señorita*.

There are no hereditary titles.

Do *not* use Señor Don or Señora Doña in Panama. Instead, old and eminent persons are addressed simply as *Don / Doña* (followed by given name). Thus: *Doña Alba*. Never use such courtesy titles with young people.

If you are unsure whether Don/Doña are appropriate, use *Señor / Señora*.

Professional titles: Someone with a degree in engineering is called *Ingeniero (m) or Ingeniera (f)*, and someone who has graduated in any subject is a *Licenciado (m) or Licenciada (f)*. A medical doctor or person with a doctorate in any discipline is a *Doctor (m) or Doctora (f)*. In oral address use the professional title followed by their father's surname. Say: *Dr. Domínguez*, or *Licenciado Domínguez*. However, write the full name.
Note that whether writing or speaking these titles replace the honorific. Do not use both.

Over-politeness is appreciated and is not out of place.

An ambassador is Señor Embajador. When writing, begin with the complete name and rank. Thus: Dr. Orlando Morales Garcia, Ministro de Turismo.

Address a Minister orally as Señor Ministro. Salutation: Estimado Señor Ministro. Refer to him in writing as Su Exclencia El Ministro.

Persons in a government agency should be addressed using their professional titles. Thus:

Written: Ing. Oral: Ingeniero Salutation: Estimado Ingeniero.

Members of parliament are addressed as *Honorable Representate*, and Members of the Supreme Court are *Señor Magistrado or Honorable Señor*.

Papua New Guinea

Mr Kuike Job NUMOI
(Big Man NUMOI)

With more than 700 languages and dialects, and many tribes, there is a highly complicated and diverse structure for forms of address..

In general, educated people use forms of address corresponding to those used in the UK. Thus: *Mr Peter Carmichael Lake EAFERE*.

Women usually adopt their husband's family name upon marriage but retain their maiden name. In correspondence, for instance, you should write to: *Mrs Josepha Eafere née Temu*.

Orally, address her as *Mrs Eafere*. However, in the pidgin English that is popularly used, she will be addressed in speech as *Misses Eafere* in the same way that Papua New Guineans refer to the Queen of England as *Missis Kween*.

Children do not necessarily take their parent's family name. They may be given the name of a warrior uncle, or perhaps of the best fisherman in the village. Therefore sisters and brothers may have entirely different names. However, among the educated the trend is now towards the English system.

There are no titles as such, but there are legions of tribes and heads of tribes, and chiefs who often acquire their titles through tests of valour, though there is no tribal structure in the African sense. They should be addressed respectfully, and the custom is to refer to them as Big Man.

Paraguay

Señora Alba DOMÍNGUEZ de Farhat

SPANISH IS SPOKEN.

See also the general chapter on Spanish American forms of address.

Mr = *Señor*   Mrs = *Señora*   Miss = *Señorita*

In correspondence abbreviate to:

Sr.   Sra.   Srta.

The given name is followed by the father's surname, then the mother's surname.

Address a man by his father's surname. Thus: *Señor Igor ALBERTO Pangrazio.*

The courtesy titles *Señor Don* or *Señora Doña* for persons of eminence are not used in Paraguay. They are considered too formal. Just say *Señora surname* (husband's) or write Dear *Señora* (husband's) *surname.*

There are no hereditary titles.

Professional titles: Someone with a degree in engineering is called *Ingeniero (m) or Ingeniera (f)*, and someone with a university degree in any subject at post graduate level is a *Licenciado (m) or Licenciada (f)*. A medical doctor or person with a doctorate in any discipline is a *Doctor (m) or Doctora (f)*. In oral address use the professional title followed by the father's surname. Thus: *Dr Alberto*.
Note that whether writing or speaking these titles replace the honorific. Do not use both.

In correspondence use *Ing., Lic., Dr.*, respectively, but begin with the professional title followed by the given name, then the father's surname, then the mother's surname. Thus: *Dr. Orlando Morales Garcia*.

A Minister is addressed orally as Señor Ministro (Minister). An ambassador is Señor Embajador. When writing, begin with the complete name and rank. Thus: *Dr. Orlando Morales García, Ministro de Turismo*.

Peru

Señor Dr Arturo GARCÍA Rodriguez

SPANISH IS SPOKEN.

See also the chapter on Spanish American forms of address.

Mr = *Señor*   Mrs = *Señora*   Miss = *Señorita*

In correspondence abbreviate to

Sr.   Sra.   Srta.

The given name is followed by the father's surname, then the mother's surname.

Address a man by his father's family name. Thus *Señor García*.

In writing, married women use *Señora* followed by the given name, father's surname, de (of), then husband's surname. However, in correspondence, use the full name and drop the "de". Orally, one would normally address and refer to a married woman by her prefered surname, e.g. *Señora Campora* or *Señora de Campora*. For verbal communication, *Señora Díaz de Campora* is too long. The same applies to unmarried women. *Srta. María García* is too long, so one would tend to say *Srta. García* in conversation.

A young unmarried woman would be addressed as *Señorita*. A more mature woman would be addressed as *Señora* whether married or not.

There are no hereditary titles.

The courtesy titles *Don* and *Doña* are used for eminent persons, though less frequently these days. Say: *Señor Don* (m) or *Señora Doña* (f) followed by the given name. Thus: *Señor Don Luis*.

However, note that *don* (with a lower case "d") is used on envelopes. Thus: *Señor don Pablo Sanchez*. Also be aware that *doña* is only used in special instances.

Do not place the honorific before *Don/a* in ordinary situations, just one or the other. Thus *Señor García* or *Don Arturo*. Usually *Señor /a* is sufficient.

In oral address use the professional title followed by the father's surname. Thus: *Dr. García*.

Use appropriate forms of address when writing or speaking to people with professional titles. Place the honorific before the courtesy titles. Thus:

Ingeniero / Ingeniera for an engineer
Arquitecto / Arquitecta for an architect
Doctor/a for a doctor or lawyer

Note that Licenciado / Licenciada is not used.

In correspondence use *Ing.*, *Dr.*, etc, but begin with the professional title followed by the given name, then the father's surname, then the mother's surname. Thus: Sr. *Dr. Orlando Morales García*.

Philippines

Mr Simeon B. ABARQUEZ

The majority of Filipinos are Christians and use forms of address corresponding largely to those used in American English. The second given name is often shortened to the initial. With unmarried women it is normally the initial of their mother's surname; with married women it is their maiden surname.

For correspondence use *Dear Sir* or *Madam*.

When addressing people with a professional degree, precede the qualification with *Mr*, *Mrs*, or *Miss*. An attorney would be addressed as *Mr Attorney* (or with the family name as Attorney Abarquez), and a person with a degree in engineering would be *Mr Engineer*. Professor and doctors should be addressed appropriately.

There are professions where the title will always be used in both formal and informal conversation and in correspondence. These are: *attorneys, engineers, doctors, professors*.

Tagalog is the national language spoken by most Filipinos. English is the formal language.

Sir or Mr = *Ginoo*   Madam or Mrs = *Ginang*   Miss = *Binibini*

In correspondence abbreviate to:

G.   Gng.   Bb.

In common with American usage, a *Minister* is a religious official, not a government official. Government ministers are called *Secretaries*, and should properly be addressed as *Mr Secretary*, though *Honorable Secretary* is often preferred. In general, the terminology for members of the administration is similar to that of the USA. Senior public officials, such as Secretaries and Mayors, tend to be addressed only by their titles, not by their names. Their wives are addressed, for example, as Mrs Mayor.

Congress comprises the House of Representatives, whose members are addressed as *Congressmen*, and the House of Senate, whose members are *Senators*. Members of both Houses are addressed as *Honourable*.

In correspondence, use: *The Honourable XYZ, Congressman from (district)*, or *The Honourable XYZ, Senator of the Philippines*. On the envelope and at the opening of the letter abbreviate Senator to *Sen.* and Congressman to *Cong.* or *Rep.* (either may be used).

Social correspondence may be ended with "Sincerely". "Respectfully Yours" is used as a complimentary form in business letters.

Older Filipinos sometimes continue to use Spanish forms of address, especially in conversation. They would also use *Don* and *Doña* (see chapter on Spain).

Although it originated in Ilocano Province, *Apo* is commonly used throughout the Philipines as a form of respect to address a man of high status in the community because of his governmental position. There is no equivalent for women. Similarly, *Lakay* is used to address a man of high status in the community. They are both used before either the first name or the family name.

Some Muslims adopt forms of address with some similarity to those of Malaysia:

A *Sultan* is the head of a clan, and a *Dato* (political title) is head of a family.

A female Muslim who is the daughter of a Dato or Sultan should be addressed as *Bai* (followed by family name).

The Son of a Sultan is addressed as *Datu*, and the son of a Datu also becomes a *Datu*.

Pitcairn Island

Forms of address correspond to those used in the UK.

Poland

Pan Romuald SZUNIEWICZ

Mr = *Pan*   Mrs = *Pani*   Miss = *use Pani*

There is no longer any distinction between Mrs and Miss. The word Panna (Miss) is now uncommon.

The given name is followed by the surname. Thus: Janusz Herczyński would be addressed as *Pan Herezyński*. Your dilemma will be not so much that of the correct form of address as one of pronunciation.

In writing, different forms may appear. For example (noun cases): Pan / Pana, Panem, etc. In Polish the formal opening for general correspondence is: *Szanowny Panie* (male) or *Szanowna Pani* (female). For business correspondence English is acceptable so it is not necessary to know these forms.

The usual ending for people's surnames is *-ski*, with the feminine form *-ska*. If the ending of the name is *-cki* the feminine form is *-cka*. Thus: Count Potocki, Countess Potocka. Certain names have the feminine form *-owa* (pronounced ova). Thus: Dubis = Dubisowa. Others are indeclinable, thus Debiec is for both sexes.

There are many expressive forms for Polish given names. Sometimes they have an endearing meaning, others denote familiarity, and some are derogatory. Thus: *Maria* may become *Marysia* as a name of familiarity, or *Marysienka* between lovers, or *Marysia* again within the family, or *Marycha* if using it in the derogatory mode, giving it a coarse intonation.

When writing, refer to a person's professional qualifications:

An engineer is addressed as: *inż.* (followed by the first and family name).

A person with an MSc is addressed as *mgr inż. (followed by the first and family name).*

For someone with a PhD. use dr (without the full stop).

There is a wide variety of hereditary titles, most of which are rarely used. One example is the use of *Hrabio!*, which may be used orally and in correspondence before the first name, which is followed by the hereditary title, then the family name. However this is generally regarded now as unfashionable.

For persons of title or rank, such as Ambassadors and Ministers, say: *Panie Ministrze (for a male Minister)*, *Pani Minister* (for a female

Minister), *Panie Ambasadorze* (for a male Ambassador) and *Pani Ambassador* (for a female Ambassador).

In correspondence, address these persons as: *Wasza Ekscelencjo!*

Polynesia (French)
Including Tahiti, Windward Islands and
Leeward Islands, with Bora Bora)

French and Tahitian are spoken throughout French Polynesia, and French forms of address should be used in the same way as in France.

    Mr = *Monsieur*   Mrs = *Madame*   Miss = *Mademoiselle*

In Tahitian say or write *Tane after the last name* (for Mr) or *Vahine* (for Mrs / Miss).

Portugal

Senhor Antonio VAZ PEIRERA

When addressing people orally:

    Mr = *Senhor*   Mrs = *Senhora, Minha Senhora, or Dona*
                Miss = *Senhora* or *Menina*

Dona can be used in directly addressing any married woman, or a mature unmarried woman.

Senhora (or for married women the politer form *Minha Senhora*) is used in direct address, but is more appropriate when *referring to* a woman.

An unmarried woman can also be addressed or referred to as *Menina*, followed by her forename.

Men usually include their mother's maiden name before their father's surname. A married woman may retain her maiden surname before her married surname.

Greet men and women always using the honorific with the last two names in the name string. Thus Francisco Manuel Seixas da Costa becomes Senhor SEIXAS da COSTA (retaining the preposition *da*).

José Duarte de Cámara Ramalho Ortigão is Senhor RAMALHO ORTIGÃO
Ana Maria Rosa Martins Gomez is Senhora MARTINS GOMEZ

When familiar, use the first Christian name plus the last of the two family names. Thus: *Ana Gomez*.

Note that there are many women with *Maria* as their Christian name so it is the custom when writing to place the second Christian name afterwards, together with the two family names. Thus: *Maria Yosé Ramalho Ortigão*.

In correspondence it is unnecessary to write all the names. Just use the honorific followed by the initials of the given names then the family names. Thus: *Senhor F. M. Seixas da Costa*.

In Portuguese, open with Dear Sir / Dear Madam by using *Exmo.* (m) or *Exma.* (f). Thus: *Exmo. Senhor*, and *Exma. Senhora*.

It is customary to address people with professional qualifications by placing the title after the honorific. Here are some examples:

Senhor Professor Seixas da Costa. (Professor is abbreviated to Prof. for ordinary schoolteachers). (Senhora Professora)

Senhor Doutor (doctor – do not abbreviate).
(Senhora Doutora)

Senhor Engenheiro (engineer).
(Senhora Engenheira)

Senhora Arquitecto (architect).
(Senhora Arquitecta).

The university and the degree should be arranged after the name. Write: Exmo. Senhor Dr., or Exmo. Senhor Arqto. etc, followed by the full name.

Those with degrees of Licenciado or Bacharel are styled *Dr*. Note that the word "Doutor" is only written in full for one with a doctorate.

A Minister is addressed orally as *Senhor Ministro / Senhora Ministra*. Similarly, an Ambassador is *Senhor Embaixador / Senhora Embaixadora*. In correspondence, write *Su Excelencia*, followed by rank.

Those with conferred titles are addressed orally as *Senhor* or *Senhora* followed by the title. Thus: Senhor Duque de (nameplace). But in written form they are addressed as Exmo. Senhor Duque de (nameplace), or Exma. Senhora Marquesa de (nameplace).

Formal correspondence to those with titles should be addressed to: *Excelentissimo Senhor, Conde de*... The envelope should be addressed: *Dom Manuel de Braganca*. Dom is restricted to a few families, but the feminine equivalent, Dona, is customarily used for all women whether married or single. The abbreviation D. is frequently used for both Dom and Dona.

Correspondence should be signed off: *de V. Exa. Atenciosamente*.

With hereditary titles, address the Duque, Marques, Conde, etc. directly. Thus: *Duque de* (nameplace).

Titles:

Príncipe de (Princesa de)
Duque de (Duquesa de)

Marques de (Marqueêsa de)
Conde de (Condessa de)
Visconde de (Viscondessa de)
Barão de (Baronesa de)

Puerto Rico

Mr (or Señor) Rubén Berrios MARTINEZ

Puerto Rico exhibits a mixture of American customs strongly flavoured by Hispanic traditions.

Although Spanish predominates, American usage is widely acceptable in business circles.

The use of first names is common in the ordinary course of business, but only after a relationship has been established. Initially use the *last name* preceded by Mr or Mrs, or you may use the following (before the *last name*):

Mr = *Señor*   Mrs = *Señora*   Miss = *Señorita*

In correspondence abbreviate to:

Sr.   *Sra.*   *Srta.*

Qatar

Sayed SAQR Mubarak Al Mansouri

See also the chapter on Arab forms of address.

Mr = *Sayed*   Mrs = *Sayeda*   Miss = *Anessa*

There are no hard and fast rules with Arab names. Everything is loose and variable, and different influences will govern the practices of each Arab country.

Within the string of Arab names everyone usually has their own given name followed by their father's given name. Thus: *Mohamad Jemal* or *Mohamad bin Jemal*. Complications arise as the string is added to by the practice of honouring ancestors.

Women also derive their names from their father, and sometimes add their father's father, and so on, ending with their family name. They retain their own names after marriage.

The full name chain that many Arabs use is for official use on documentation only, for example, for passports and marriage certificates. Otherwise, it is not necessary to refer to them all.

In correspondence the rules are again variable. Use business cards as a clue.

Some surnames are derived from tribes as a matter of family policy. The root name (i.e. the last name) is often a description of ancestors, a tribal name, or a place.

Example of the derivation of the name string of a male, Ali Abdullah Mughram Al-Ghamdi:

Given name	Father's name	Grandfather's name	Surname, perhaps tribal name
Ali	Abdullah	Mughram	Al-Ghamdi

"Al" and "El" mean "tribe of".

So you will tend always to find a person's given name and always the name of their father, frequently also their grandfather's name, then their tribal-type name, which often, but not always, is preceded by "Al".

The same principle applies to men and to women.

In oral address all that matters will depend entirely on the relationship between the parties.

Generally, people do not call someone only by their first names except between close social friends. They will always use the honorific before the given name when addressing each other at work. Thus, using the example of the name string above, he would be addressed simply as Sayed Ali.

In correspondence it is usual, but not the rule, to use the honorific followed by the given name, father's name, and last name. Thus: Sayed Ali Abdullah Al-Ghamdi. Therefore, if any names are to be left out, they should be those sandwiched between the father's name and the final name in the string.

Titles are very important. Therefore in correspondence address an engineer as: Engineer Ali Al-Ghamdi. This also applies to lawyers and doctors. Sometimes it may be stretched to include accountants and architects, but there is no firm rule.

In oral address too, use the full professional title. On subsequent mention one should say simply "Engineer", or "Doctor", etc.

When corresponding to a married lady it is customary with many households to do so via the husband.

A single female whose name is Taibah Atallah El-Garny would be addressed informally (and orally) by acquaintances as Anessa Taibah, but formally as Anessa El-Garny.

In correspondence she would be addressed as Anessa Taibah El-Garny.

All members of the Qatari royal family have the family name Al-Thani and are addressed as Sheikh (m) or Sheikha (f), as with: *H.H. Sheikh Khalifa Bin Hamad Al-Thani*, the Amir. He is referred to as *Sheikh Khalifa*. This is the only title in Qatar. There is only one Amir.

Réunion

Forms of address in Réunion are the same as those used in France. See the chapter on France for more details.

Mr = *Monsieur*   Mrs = *Madame*   Miss = *Mademoiselle*

Romania

Domnul Gheorghe MARIN

When speaking to Mr Marin, he should be addressed as *"Domnule Marin"* (first name, Gheorghe, is not mentioned.)

When writing to Mr Marin, he should be addressed as "Domnul Gheorghe Marin" (no "e" after "Domnul"), or "Dl. Gheorghe Marin" (in the address), and at the beginning of the letter as "Stimate domn" "Dear Sir"). Similarly, Mrs and Miss at the beginning of a letter should be "Stimată doamnă" and "Stimată domnişoară".

Oral forms of address:

Mr = *Domnule*   Mrs = *Doamnă*   Miss = *Domnişoară*
    (when addressing a person unknown to the speaker)

or

Mr = *Domnule*   Mrs = *Doamna*   Miss = *Domnişoara*
(when followed by the person's surname (e.g. Domnule Marin)

The following terms are used in correspondence (in the address only):

Mr = *Domnul*   Mrs = *Doamna*   Miss = *Domnişoara*

Abbreviations used in correspondence (in the address only):

Mr = *Dl*   Mrs = *D-na*   Miss = *D-ra*

Most wives adopt their husband's surname on marriage, some use both their own and their husband's, and a few retain their maiden name.

There are no hereditary or conferred titles.

When writing or speaking to officials use the honorific before the title, e.g. *Mr Secretary of State*, Mr Director General.

Russia

Gospodin Anatoli Nikolaevich NAZAROV
or ANATOLI NIKOLAEVICH

Mr = *Gospodin*   Mrs/Miss = *Gospozha*

There is no distinction between married and unmarried women.

With Russian names, the forename comes first, then the patronymic, which shows filiation to the father, then the surname, which is passed on down the generations. Thus: Ivan Ivanovitch Tolstoy (m) would be addressed orally as *Ivan Ivanovitch*. In Tatiana Ivanovna (f), *Ivanovna* is the feminine patronymic of Ivan.

The Russian patronymic is formed by adding "son of" or "daughter of" to the father's name. This is expressed in the above examples by the use of *-ovitch* and *-ovna* respectively. Patronymics are usually contracted in actual speech (*Ivanovitch* might be called *Ivanitch*). With some names, however, the construction makes contraction (abbreviation) impossible.

Honorifics are usually reserved for use with foreigners and are generally omitted between Russians conversing with one another. When used, honorifics precede the surname alone. Thus: *Gospodin Tolstoy*.

Foreigners, however, should generally address Russians according to local custom by using just the forename together with the patronymic (*Ivan Ivanovitch*). The forename and patronymic should certainly be used in formal situations, thereby omitting the family name. So when talking *to* a person, use only the forename and the patronymic. Thus: *Ivan Ivanovitch* (without the honorific). If talking *about* someone you can use the surname as a means of identification.

Exceptionally, when addressing persons of rank or with a professional qualification you should use only the surname. Thus: Ivan Ivanovitch Tolstoy would be addressed as *Professor Tolstoy*.

The patronymic is often used among men on its own as a term of familiarity. Thus: *Petrovitch*.

When speaking to a youngster, or when youngsters speak to one another, using just the forename is acceptable.

Some women adopt their husband's family name upon marriage. It is also common to hyphenate their married and maiden family names.

Correspondence should be addressed using the initial of the first name followed by the family name (ignoring the patronymic). Thus: *Sergei Ivanovitch Ivanov* would become *S. Ivanov*.

Unless a name has a foreign origin, when it is indeclinable, the feminine form of *-ski* (meaning "of") becomes *-skaya*. Similarly with *-skoy*. Thus: *Trubetskoy, Trubetskaya*.

Many families who have settled outside Russia forgo the feminine ending.

Russian surnames bear a stress on a particular syllable, which is important for the pronunciation. The problem is that the stress is not on the same syllable in each name. There are no hard and fast rules, so you will need a good ear.

There are many expressive forms for Russian given names. Sometimes they have an endearing meaning, others denote familiarity, and some are derogatory. Thus: *Tatiana* may become *Tania* as a name of familiarity, or *Tanyechka* between friends, or *Tanyushka* within the family, or *Tanka* if using it in the derogatory mode.

Friends call each other by their first names only, using a diminutive. Thus: *Mikhail* may become *Misha*. This is informal and unsuitable for business purposes. The cue for becoming more familiar in terms of address should be left to your Russian acquaintance.

The use of *Tovarich* (Comrade) as a form of address is becoming a relic, though some die-hards endeavour to preserve it. *Tovarich* is gender-neutral and tends, when used these days, to be in correspondence more than in conversation.

Your Excellency (instead of Comrade/*Tovarich*) is now used when addressing high functionaries.

Rwanda

Monsieur François NGARUKIYINTWALI

Mr = *Monsieur*   Mrs = *Madame*   Miss = *Mademoiselle*

Kinyarwanda is the language of Rwanda, but French is spoken in the towns and is the language of administration.

UK forms of address are also widely acceptable.

The family name appears last in the name string. Take a deep breath.

San Marino

Signor Ottaviano ROSSI

Forms of address correspond to those used in Italy.

Mr = *Signor(e)*   Mrs = *Signora*   Miss = *Signorina*

Refer to the chapter on Italy for more details.

São Tomé & Principe

Senhor ANTÓNIO de Lima Viegas

Portuguese is spoken. Use Portuguese forms of address.

Mr = *Senhor*   Miss / Mrs = *Senhora*

Address people with the honorific followed by their *first name.*

Saudi Arabia

Sayed ZEYAD Anad Mahmoud Al-Gheraiyedh

See also the chapter on Arab forms of address.

Mr = *Sayed*   Mrs = *Sayeda*   Miss = *Anessa*

There are no hard and fast rules with Arab names. Everything is loose and variable, and different influences will govern the practices of each Arab country.

Within the string of Arab names everyone usually has their own given name followed by their father's given name. Thus: Mohamad Jemal or Mohamad bin Jemal. Complications arise as the string is added to by the practice of honouring ancestors.

Women also derive their names from their father, and sometimes add their father's father, and so on, ending with their family name. They retain their own names after marriage.

The full name chain that many Arabs use is for official use on documentation only, for example, for passports and marriage certificates. Otherwise, it is not necessary to refer to them all.

In correspondence the rules are again variable. Use business cards as a clue.

Some surnames are derived from tribes as a matter of family policy. The root name (i.e. the last name) is often a description of ancestors, a tribal name, or a place.

Example of the derivation of the name string of a male, Ali Abdullah Mughram Al-Ghamdi:

Given name	Father's name	Grandfather's name	Surname, perhaps tribal name
Ali	Abdullah	Mughram	Al-Ghamdi

"Al" and "El" mean "tribe of".

So you will tend always to find a person's given name and always the name of their father, frequently also their grandfather's name, then their tribal-type name, which often, but not always, is preceded by "Al".

The same principle applies to men and to women.

196

In oral address all that matters will depend entirely on the relationship between the parties.

Generally, people do not call someone only by their first names except between close social friends. They will always use the honorific before the given name when addressing each other at work. Thus, using the example of the name string above, he would be addressed simply as Sayed Ali.

In correspondence it is usual, but not the rule, to use the honorific followed by the given name, father's name, and last name. Thus: *Sayed Ali Abdullah Al-Ghamdi.* Therefore, if any names are to be left out, they should be those sandwiched between the father's name and the final name in the string.

Titles are very important. Therefore in correspondence address an engineer as: *Engineer Ali Al-Ghamdi.* This also applies to lawyers and doctors. Sometimes it may be stretched to include accountants and architects, but there is no firm rule.

In oral address too, use the full professional title. On subsequent mention one should say simply "Engineer", or "Doctor", etc.

When corresponding to a married woman it is customary with many households to do so via the husband.

A single woman whose name is Taibah Atallah El-Garny would be addressed informally (and orally) by acquaintances as *Anessa Taibah*, but formally as *Anessa El-Garny*.

In correspondence she would be addressed as *Anessa Taibah El-Garny*.

In Saudi Arabia Sheikh is a traditional title that was bestowed on prominent families by the royal family, but it is now considered an ancient title and is no longer given. Nowadays, such families are addressed in the ordinary way. Nor are tribal leaders referred to as *Sheikh*.

There are numerous princes and princesses. They are addressed as *Amir* (prince) and *Amira* (princess).

Senegal

Monsieur Mouhamadou Lamine DIAGNE

Use French forms of address.

Mr = *Monsieur*   Mrs = *Madame*   Miss = *Mademoiselle*

A director of a company should be addressed as *Monsieur le directeur*, and a Minister as *Monsieur le ministre*.

Seychelles

Msye William HERMINIE

The official languages are Creole, English, and French, with almost everyone speaking Creole.

English forms of address are widely used in the same way as in the UK and are generally used for correspondence.

French forms of address may be used orally but *Mademoiselle* is not used. It is preferrable to use Creole – a French patois:

WHEN USING CREOLE:

Mr = *Msye*   Mrs = *Madam*   Miss = *Ms*

The family name is always last in the name string.

Sierra Leone

Mr Gibril SAMURA

Although there are 12 tribes, and several of them employ multiple dialects, forms of address as those in the UK are widely used.

Informality is acceptable, and people usually are addressed by their first name. Thus: Abdul Hassan Kamara would be addressed orally as *Abdul*. In correspondence address him as *Mr Abdul Kamara*.

Women take their husband's name upon marriage.

A tribal chief is known as *Kandeh*. Thus: *Kandeh Bockarie*. Tribal chiefs and elders should then be addressed respectfully as *Sir*.

The hereditary title *Pa Alimami* is applied to a sectioni chief or town chief. Thus: *Pa Alimami Kamara*.

Singapore

Miss LEE Lay See (Chinese)

In this multicultural island state the unacquainted foreigner must contend with different forms of address for each community. This comprises mainly the Chinese majority and the Malay and Indian minorities.

Chinese

When addressing Chinese, note that names usually are divided into three monosyllables. Thus: *Ng Kiap Khee*. You should address him as *Mr Ng*, *Ng* being the family name.

When there is a measure of familiarity, Mr Ng may be addressed orally simply as *Ng*, which he will reciprocate by addressing you by your own family name without the honorific. You may find this somewhat disarming, as if summoning an errant schoolchild, but no offence is intended. When you have developed a stronger relationship you may advance to first name terms. You would therefore address Mr Ng as *Kiap Khee*, remembering to compound both names as one.

The custom of addressing someone by their family name without honorific does not extend to women. Thus: *Lee Lay See* would be *Mrs/Miss Lee*, or *Lay See*, but not *Lee*.

The religious divides within the Chinese community have no effect on these customs. However, some older married women may prefer to be addressed as *Madam*.

It has become commonplace for Chinese Singaporeans to adopt a Western forename whilst retaining their traditional names. Thus, *Harry Ng Kiap Khee* may be addressed as *Mr Ng* (formal), *Harry* (informal), and *Mr Harry Ng* (written form). In this case there is no need to use the full Chinese name.

There are some Chinese who adopt aliases. This often signifies that there has been bad luck in the past, and a new name will carry a change of fortune. The original names may not be evident, though some people do use both on their stationery. In very formal proceedings a person who uses an alias should be addressed in written form as (for instance) *Ng Guat Hoon, alias Chai Yen Fatt*. Otherwise, address him or her by the newest name only. Some people consider it bad form to refer to the former names.

See also the note on dialects in the chapter on China.

Indian

The Indian community is divided religiously between Hindus, Muslims, Sikhs, Parses, and Christians. There are also Tamils, though Tamil is not a religion, but a regional ethnic group with its own language.

Except for the Muslim Indian community, for whom one should sometimes apply forms of address used by Malays (see chapter on Malaysia), Western forms of address should be used. Thus: Mr Thiagarajah THIRUNAGAN (Hindu).

Tamil Hindus in particular have long forenames which are often abbreviated, and the shortened form is acceptable in both written and oral usage. Thus *Subramaniam Damodara Pakirisamy* is short-ened to *Mr S.D.P. Samy*, where the application of the final initial *P* is deliberate.

Within the *Sikh* community every male has the name *Singh* (mean-ing Lion) after his given name. Thus: *Manjit Singh Gill*. Similarly, every female *Sikh* has the name *Kaur* (meaning Princess) after her given name, which, too, may be followed by the clan name. Thus: *Ranjit Kaur Dhillon*. She would then be addressed either as *Ms Kaur* or *Ms Dhillon*.

An interesting feature of *Sikh* names is that both male and female can have the same given name distinguished only by *Singh* or *Kaur*, as with *Daljit Singh Gill* and *Daljit Kaur Gill*.

Within the local Sikh community an adult male or female is addressed as *Sardar or Sardarnee* respectively instead of Mr or Ms. Male children are addressed as *Kaka*, and female as *Bibi*. Thus: *Sardar Beant Singh*; *Sardarnee Beant Kaur*; *Kaka Beant Singh*; and *Bibi Beant Kaur* respectively.

However, the name *Singh* is also used by the *Rajputs*, a warrior race from Northwest India who are Hindus, for their first-born son (e.g.

Rajiv Singh). There is no parallel for the use of *Kaur* for the female Rajput.

Malay

When addressing Malays, who are Muslims, adopt the practice applying to Malaysia (see Malaysia chapter), but note that there are no bestowed or hereditary titles in Singapore.

Tip: Singapore is a status-conscious society, but status is defined in terms of academic and personal achievement, not social class. At the same time wealth commands respect. The most senior person present at a meeting commands the most respect and in negotiations is often the one given the most say.

Slovak Republic

Pán Juraj VALL

Mr = *Pán*   Mrs = *Pani*   Miss = *Slečna*
(abbreviate Slečňa to Sl. in correspondence)
Pani may be used if it is unclear whether the woman is married.

The family name appears last in the name string. Thus Vladimír Devečka is addressed as *Pán Devečka*, as with most Western countries.

The majority of women (about 70%) suffix *-ova* to their family name as a feminine close, so Mr Devečka's wife would be *Pani Devečkova*.

The patronymic system does not apply to the Slovak Republic.

Professional titles are used before the given and family name when writing, or before the family name when speaking. A selection:

	Masc.	Fem.	Abbrev. to when writing
Doctor of medicine	Doktor	Doktora	Mudr. or Dr.
Engineer	Inzinier	Inzinierka	Ing.
Lawyer	Pravnik	Pravnička	JUDr. or Dr.

People with Bachelor and Master degrees tend now to be addressed in writing with the English initials BA / MA etc. after their name.

Slovenia

Gospod Bozo CERAR

Forms of address in Slovenia correspond largely to those used in the UK, with the family name appearing last.

Mr = *Gospod*   Mrs = *Gospa*   Miss = *Gospodicna*

In correspondence abbreviate to:

G.   Ga.   Gca.

Thus: *G. Joze Breznik* (Mr) – *Ga Marija Breznik* (Mrs)

Women usually adopt their husband's name upon marriage, but not always.

Married women sometimes have feminized surnames (for instance: *Mr Petrov* and *Mrs Petrova*), but it is also proper to address women orally or in writing by omitting the feminine ending.

Recognise persons with professional qualifications by addressing them as such. The title is deemed to be a personal attachment to the given name(s) (instead of the family name), but this has an effect on its use, which is before the given name and family name (when writing) or before the family name (in conversation). Here are selected examples:

Note that for the majority of cases the masculine form is used whether the person is male or female.

Engineer = Inzenir, abbreviate when writing to *dipl. ing.*
Architect = *Arhitekt*, abbreviate when writing to *dipl. arch.* (which is usually followed by the faculty becaue there are different disciplines)
Doctor   = *Doktor*, abbreviate when writing to *Dr.*
Lawyer   = *Jurist* (or sometimes *Iurist*), abbreviate when writing to *dipl. iur*,.

Solomon Islands

Mr Lindsay F. MISROS

Forms of address correspond largely to those used in the UK, with some Australian trespass.

Whilst there are no hereditary titles, a person's name signifies his/ her line of descent from the tribal Chiefs, but there is no special form of address.

There are conferred titles entitling people to be addressed as *Sir*, such as holders of KCMG, etc, just as in the UK. Similarly, persons of rank are addressed appropriately. Thus:

The Governor General is addressed as Your Excellency, and the Chief Justice is addressed as The Honourable (then all names).

Somalia

AHMED Ali

Honorifics are not used in Somalia. There are no equivalents to Mr, Mrs, or Miss in the vernacular, though foreigners may tend to use English honorifics out of habit.

People are addressed by their first name. So address Ahmed Ali as *Ahmed*.

Names are Arabic in structure and usually comprise two disclosed names plus a third that is not generally used. The first name is the given name, the second is often a nickname, and the undisclosed third name is the family name, which is the father's first name.

Women retain their maiden names and are not addressed as *Mrs*. Instead, and if you are speaking or writing in English, say (or write) *Madame*. Madame may be used alone, but if you are addressing the woman by name, use the first name. In the vernacular they would not use an honorific, just the first name.

South Africa

Mr Kent Durr

There are 11 languages, but English and Afrikaans are the languages used for business and by the courts. UK forms of address are widely used in government circles.

Zulu, Sutmo, Xhosa, and Tswana are the most widely *spoken* languages, but English forms of address are usually appropriate.

However, there are some people who prefer not to be addressed in Afrikaans and others who prefer Afrikaans over English. The equivalents of Mr, Mrs, and Miss in Afrikaans are Mnr, Mev, and Mej respectively.

Below is a summary of the correct forms of address in English for persons in office:

Position	Open	End	Say
State President	Dear President, or Dear State President	Yours most respectfully	Mr State President (and subsequently President)
Chief Justice	Your Honour, or Dear Mr Chief Justice (and Mrs XYZ)	Yours respectfully	Judge, or Sir (in court)
Cabinet Ministers, Ministers of Ministers' Councils, and Deputy Ministers	Dear Mr Minister etc, or Dear Sir, or Dear Minister & Mrs XYZ	Yours respectfully	Mr Minister (etc), then Sir
Ambassador	Your Excellency *or* Mr Ambassador *or* Dear Mr Ambassador	Yours respectfully (*for the public, thus not official language*)	Mr Ambassador *or* Your Excellency *then* Sir (wife = Mrs XYZ)
Member of Parliament	Sir/Madam *or* Dear Mr (and Mrs) XYZ	Yours respectfully	Mr XYZ *or* Sir/Madam

South Georgia and South Sandwich Islands

Forms of address correspond to those used in the UK.

Spain

Señor Don Federico TORRES Muro

See also the introductory chapter on Spanish-American forms of Address.

Mr = *Señor*   Mrs = *Señora*   Miss = *Señorita*

In correspondence abbreviate to:

Sr.   *Sra.*   *Srta.*

A man's family name is often followed by his mother's maiden name, as with the above example, where *Señor* is the honorific, *Don* is the courtesy title, *Frederico* is the forename (given or Christian name), his family name (father's name) is *Torres*, and his mother's maiden name is *Muro*.

When speaking or opening a letter address someone as (using the masculine as our example, though the feminine rule is the same):

Señor Torres

when addressing an envelope use:

Señor Don Frederico Torres

All are correct, though the first example is informal and probably less appropriate for business purposes.

The courtesy title *Don* (and *Doña* for women) is a customary form of respect, used on envelopes etc. as above, or occasionally in conversation with just the given name.

The full name string usually appears on business cards.

A married woman may also be addressed by her maiden surname, with her husband's attached, e.g. *Sra. Dona María Luisa* (then maiden name) de (then husband's surname).

Señora is followed by de (of) before the surname on the envelope and in correspondence, but de is dropped in oral address.

If a husband and wife are addressed jointly, his full name is given before his wife's, e.g. *Señor Don Juan Lopez* and *Señora de Lopez*.

In writing (only), an unmarried woman is addressed in full, for instance as *Señorita Doña María Luisa* (followed by surname).

Unlike most of Latin America, Spain does not address those with academic qualifications with any particular deference. Therefore do *not* use *Licenciado*, *Ingeniero*, etc. The only exception is with *Doctor/a*.

Titles are still conferred.

All Duques, some Marqués and Condes, and a few Viscondes are Grandees of Spain. All Grandees and their consorts are in English addressed as *Excellency*.

Ambassadors, Generals, Bishops, the holders of Grand Crosses of various Orders, and the eldest sons of Grandees together with their wives, are also addressed as *Excellency*.

An envelope to an Excellency should be addressed as: *Excelentísimo Señor*, usually abbreviated to *Exmo*. Sr. followed by his title. If he has no title, follow with the courtesy title *Don*. Thus: *Excmo. Sr. General Don*, then forename and surname.

Married women are addressed similarly as *Excelentísima Señora*, usually abbreviated to *Excma. Sra.*

Nobles who are not Grandees are addressed in writing as *El Visconde de . . .*

Titles:

Príncipe de (Princesa de)
Duque de (Duquesa de)
Marqués de (Marquesa de)
Conde de (Condesa de)
Visconde de (Vizcondesa de)
Barón de (Baronesa de)

Sri Lanka

Mr Gamini ATHUKORALE

Whether you are addressing a Sinhalese, Burgher, Tamil, or Muslim, the family is the last name, and everyone is addressed as Mr, Mrs, or Miss Lastname. Forms of address in Sri Lanka correspond to those used in the UK regardless of the community.

There is much informality and people often omit the honorific

Women take their husband's family name upon marriage.

There are many titles, but they have no bearing on greetings and foreigners need not use them.

Many people have a "silent" ancestral name, as with the following example. Fortunately, this is commonly expressed in correspondence simply by use of its initial. It is not referred to at all in spoken forms of address. Address the person below simply as *Mr Cooray*.

ancestral name	given name	surname
Pesteruweliyanaralalage	Evans	Cooray

St Helena

(including Ascension and Tristan da Cunha)

Forms of address correspond to those used in the UK.

Sudan

Sayed ALI Mohamed Osman Yassin

See also the chapter on Arab forms of address.

Mr = *Sayed*   Mrs = *Sayeda*   Miss = *Anessa*

There are no hard and fast rules with Arab names. Everything is loose and variable, and different influences will govern the practices of each Arab country.

In Sudan the general practice, whether orally or in correspondence, is to use the honorific with the first name only. Thus: Mohamed Hassan Osman will be addressed as Sayed Mohamed, and with the example at the chapter heading it will be Sayed Ali.

However, it is worthwhile repeating some details already provided for other Arab countries:

Within the string of Arab names everyone usually has their own given name followed by their father's given name.

Women also derive their names from their father, and sometimes add their father's father, and so on, ending with their family name. They retain their own names after marriage.

The full name chain that many Arabs use is for official use on documentation only, for example, for passports and marriage certificates. Otherwise, it is not necessary to refer to them all.

Some surnames are derived from tribes as a matter of family policy. The root name (i.e. the last name) is often a description of ancestors, a tribal name, or a place.

Example of the derivation of the name string of a male, Ali Abdullah Mughram El-Ghamdi:

Given name	Father's name	Grandfather's name	Surname, perhaps tribal name
Ali	Abdullah	Mughram	Al-Ghamdi

"El" means "tribe of".

So you will tend always to find a person's given name and always the name of their father, frequently also their grandfather's name, then their tribal-type name, which often, but not always, is preceded by "El".

The same principle applies to men and to women.

In oral address all that matters will depend entirely on the relationship between the parties.

Generally, people do not call someone only by their first names except between close social friends. They will always use the honorific before the given name when addressing each other at work. Thus, using the example of the name string above, he would be addressed simply as Sayed Ali.

In correspondence it is usual, but not the rule, to use the honorific followed by the given name, father's name, and last name. Thus: Sayed Ali Abdullah El-Ghamdi. Therefore, if any names are to be left out, they should be those sandwiched between the father's name and the final name in the string.

Titles are very important.

Therefore in correspondence address an engineer as: Engineer Ali El-Ghamdi. This also applies to lawyers and doctors. Sometimes it may be stretched to include accountants and architects, but there is no firm rule.

In oral address too, use the full professional title. On subsequent mention one should say simply "Engineer", or "Doctor", etc.

When corresponding to a married woman it is customary with many households to do so via the husband.

A single female whose name is Taibah Atallah El-Garny would be addressed informally (and orally) by acquaintances as Anessa Taibah, but formally as Anessa El-Garny.

In correspondence she would be addressed as Anessa Taibah El-Garny.

Suriname

De Heer Cyril Bisoendat RAMKISOR

Dutch is the official language and there are three English-related Creoles as the common vernaculars. Both Dutch and UK forms of address are used.

In Dutch:

Mr = *De Heer*   Mrs = *Mevrouw*   Miss = *Mejuffrouw*

The family name appears last in the name string.

Swaziland

Babe Mboni N. DLAMINI

For business purposes it is sufficient to use English for forms of address. Thus: Clement Themba Mabuza is addressed as *Mr Mabuza* and his wife Maziza would also be *Mrs Mabuza*.

It is not a formal society and the conduct of salutary greeting and form of address is relaxed.

The use of a European forename is not universal. Mr Mabuza's second forename, Themba, is a Swazi name meaning "hope".

Married women assume their husband's family name upon marriage.

It is not necessary to refer to a person's profession when addressing them except for doctors of medicine.

In the vernacular, Swazis prefix the titles Babe and Make to the family name. *Babe* (say barbay) literally means "father", but is used as a term of respect. Similarly, Make means mother. Thus: *Make Mabuza*.

Another local custom is to attach La to the first name when addressing women. Thus: *LaMaziza*. There is no distinction between married and unmarried women.

Swaziland is a constitutional monarchy. Hereditary titles are confined to the Royal line of accession and to the Chieftaincy. Chiefs are appointed by the King, whose first-born son usually succeeds to the title if the King agrees. A Chief is usually addressed as *Sikhulu*, though *Babe* (then family name) is acceptable.

If the Chief is a member of the royal family then address him by his first name only. Thus: Maweni Simelane would be *Chief Maweni*, alternatively: *Babe Maweni*.

A village Headman, who ranks below a Chief, is an *Induna*, but is also referred to in speech as *Babe* (but with family name).

Government ministers are addressed as *Babe* (with family name) within the local community. Foreigners should use the conventional *Honourable Minister*.

Sweden

Mr Lennart ECKERBERG

Orally and in correspondence:

$$Mr = Herr \qquad Mrs = Fru \qquad Miss = Fröken$$

In correspondence you may abbreviate to:

$$Hr. \text{ (very rare)} \qquad Fru \qquad Frk.$$

There is no oral equivalent to Ms, but the abbreviation Fr. can be used in correspondence for either Fru and Fröken.

A married woman may either drop her maiden name and adopt that of her husband, or tag her husband's name on to her own, or keep her maiden name.

Titles have become less important and the number of people on whom they are bestowed is relatively small. A Duke is *Hertig* in

Swedish, and a Duchess is *Hertriginna*, but it is not important to know such titles, as they are often not used.

When speaking or writing to government ministers etc.:

Statsrådet + Surname
Street
Town

Greeting phrase at the beginning of a letter:
Bäste herr statsråd (or minister) + surname

or in case of a woman (married or not):
Bästa fru statsråd (or minister) + surname

If you know what kind of minister the person is i.e. "*finansminister*", you can use that title. Today "*statsråd*" is the more commonly used title for cabinet ministers in Sweden.

To address verbally say: *Statsrådet + surname*

For female ambassador sometimes also: *Madam ambassadör.*

The same applies to military officers:
Bäste herr general

When writing to directors of large companies:
Direktör + surname

When speaking to directors of large companies:
Herr or direktör + surname

Apart from doctors and professors, professional titles are rarely used, although the directors of large industrial companies are often addressed as Herr Direktör (alone or with family name).

Switzerland

Monsieur Franz E. MUHEIM

Four official languages and forms of address apply to Switzerland, depending on the cantons you are visiting or writing to. Some cantons, such as Berne, Valais, and Frieborg, speak both French and German.

The dominant language is German, used by 70% of the population, and the forms of address correspond to those used in Germany. However, the spoken German in Switzerland is a difficult dialect and is only a *spoken language*.

French is spoken by 20%. The principal difference from France is with correspondence – address people by their first name and surname, in that order.

Italian is spoken by 9%, in Ticino and a couple of valleys in the canton of Graubunden. Use Italian forms of address.

Rhaeto-Romansh is used by 1%. For practical purposes you can ignore the Rhaeto-Romansh. Swiss officials advise that the language has "incomprehensible forms of address".

Thankfully, UK forms of address are widely acceptable throughout the country.

GERMAN:	*Herr(n)* (Hans MÜLLER)*	*Frau . . .*	*Fräulein . . .*
FRENCH:	*Monsieur . . .*	*Madame . . .*	*Mademoiselle . . .*
ITALIAN:	*Signor. . .*	*Signora. . .*	*Signorina . . .*

GERMAN	*Herr(n)* Doktor*	*Herr(n)* Direktor*
FRENCH	*Monsieur le docteur*	*Monsieur le directeur*
ITALIAN:	*Dottor(e)†*	*Direttore*

GERMAN:	*Herr(n)** *(Hans Müller), Direktor*
FRENCH:	*Monsieur (Hans (Müller), Directeur*
ITALIAN:	*Signore (Hans Müller), Direttore*

* Herr when referring to the person, Herrn when addressing them.

† Dottor when followed by name, Dottore when used alone.

In correspondence, write:

GERMAN:	Sehr geehrter herr Direktor
FRENCH:	Monsieur le directeur
ITALIAN:	Egregio Direttore

When corresponding to people with professional qualifications, write:

GERMAN:	Herr Hans Müller, Ingenieur
FRENCH:	Monsieur Hans Müller, Ing.
ITALIAN:	Signor Hans Müller, Ing.

Syria

Sayyed MOHAMMAD Ghassan Adel Qodmani

Refer to the chapter on Arab names for further information.

In formal oral address a person is called by his/her first name only, preceded by *Sayyed* (Mr), *Sayyedeh* (Mrs.), or *Anessah* (Miss.) You may informally address a person by using just his/her first name.

A person is known by their first and family names. It is not unusual for men to have compound first names. In the name example above, *Godmani* is the family name. Thus: *Mohammad-Ghassan Qodmani*. Women do not have compound first names.

In informal oral address the following variations are also used:

If not on a first name basis:

Akh (brother) + first name only
or *Ukht* (sister) + first name only

Similarly, if the addressee is older:

Am (uncle) alone, or *Khaleh* (aunt) alone.

If the addressee is known to have made a pilgrimage to Mecca, address him as *Haj* (pilgrim) – the word stands alone.

In formal written address use his/her first name and family name preceded by:

As-Sayyed (Mr)
As-Sayyedeh (Mrs)
Al-Anessah (Miss)

In formal written address, and particularly in official and legal application, a person's father's name, preceded by *Bin* (son of), is always placed between the first name and the family name.

Thus:

Ghassan Bin Mohammad-Adel Godmani,
or, Mohammad Ghassan Bin Adel Godmani,
or, Mohammad-Ghassan Bin Mohammad-Adel Godmani.

In formal oral address to professional people:

Doctour (doctor) + first name only if a medical practitioner.
Muhandes (engineer) + first name only.
Ustath (teacher) + first name only if a teacher or lawyer.

In formal written address to persons with professions:

al-Doctour + first and family names.
al-Muhandes + first and family names.
al-Ustath + first and family names.

Taiwan (Republic of)

Mrs GU Sze-tu

Name structures are similar to those of the People's Republic of China. The principal difference is that, when written in romanised form, the two given names are usually written as compound names, as with Hsieh Ou-yang.

The family name precedes the given name. Thus Zhu Zu-shou should be addressed as *Mr Zhu*, and Gu Jing-xian would be *Miss* or *Mrs Gu*. When informality is appropriate, address them as *Zu-shou* and *Jing-xian* respectively.

If a woman's name comprises three Chinese characters, the convention in Taiwan has been to add her own family name to her husband's family name upon marriage, thereby having four characters. Thus when *Chiu Ya-chun* (three characters) marries Mr Chang she becomes *Chang Chiu Ya-chun*, and is addressed as *Mrs Chang*. However the trend among the younger generation is now away from this (so she would continue to be *Miss Chiu*). Exceptionally, some people have names comprising two or four characters anyway. Someone with two might adopt this custom, but someone with four would not.

See also the note on dialects under China.

Tajikistan

Agha Dalwat Khudanazar

Forms of address are submitting to a slow transformation as people distance themselves from the familiar Russian patronymic system. Refer to the chapter on Russia. Using names in characteristic Russian style remains widespread because identity cards, passports, and official documents remain in that form. You should ask people how they prefer to be addressed.

59% of the population are Tajik, 23% Uzbek, 11% Russian, 7% Tatar, Kyrgyz, and Turkmen. 86% of the population are Muslim.

Although Russian forms of address, such as Gospodin (Mr) and Gospozha (Mrs/Miss) are understood, it is more suitable to use the Tajik forms Agha or Muhtaram (Mr) and Khanum (Mrs/Miss).

There is no distinction between married and unmarried women.

Occasionally one comes across patronymic names. However, people are usually addressed by their first name and father's name, as with Layeq Shirali, where Layeq is the son of Shirali.

Tanzania
(and Zanzibar)

Bwana Samuel Kaani MTALI

The dominant language on the mainland is Swahili, even in business circles. The family name is the last name in the name string.

In Swahili:

Mr Mchumo	= *Bwana Mchumo*
Mrs Mchumo	= *Bibi Mchumo*
Miss Mchumo	= *Bi Mchumo* (or Ms, in correspondence)
Dr (medical)	= *Daktari*
Dr (philosophy)	= *Dakta*

In the coastal areas men usually address one another by their first name. Thus Simba Yahya (m) would be *Bwana Simba*. In the towns people are addressed by their last name.

Moreover, in the coastal areas it is considered rude to address women by their own names. Instead, they are commonly addressed as *Mama* (mother) followed by their son's or daughter's first name. Thus: *Mama Ali* (m) or *Mama Khadija* (f). If the woman has a number of children, the choice of names will be abundant. If she has none, or if she is unmarried, address her by her last name, using the usual honorific.

Traditions are changing, and women are now increasingly adopting their husband's family name upon marriage. They are addressed as *Mama* followed by their husband's family name.

There are many clan names. For instance, several thousand people in the North might be known as *Lyimo*. In such circumstances one distinguishes the person wants to speak to by using their full name string.

Eminent personalities are addressed as *Mheshimiwa* plus family name. Government ministers and officials are addressed as *Ndugu* before the family name. These are courtesy titles equivalent in meaning to "Honourable".

Zanzibar

Whilst Tanzania comprises a majority of Christians, Zanzibar is 96% Muslim, having been governed by Omani Sultans under a

British Protectorate. Consequently people have Islamic names. The custom is to address people by their first name. Thus Seif Sharif Hamad should be addressed as *Bwana Seif*. Unlike in the Gulf countries, people do not use *bin* (son of) in their formal name string, though occasionally it may be applied orally.

The custom changes when corresponding. The correct form of address is to use the full name string or just the last name. Thus: *Bwana Hamad*. This will distinguish the person from the many others with the same first names.

Sheikh and *Maallim* are also used as terms of respect for particularly learned men. They usually precede the first name in oral address, but can be used before the full name string for oral address and correspondence.

Mzee is used similarly when addressing a man senior in age or authority.

Thailand

Khun TONGCHAN Jotikasthira

Greet people with a *wai* (palms clasped together, as if in prayer), and say *Sawasdee Khrap* (if you are male), or *Sawasdee Kha* (if you are female). This is just a polite welcome, such as "How do you do", and is provided here exceptionally because it is a variable form of address.

The honorific "Khun" is neutral and applies to men and women alike. Therefore, Mr, Mrs, Miss are all addressed as Khun, followed by the first name.

The family name is the last name, and is carried down through the generations. But it is not used in spoken forms of address except on formal occasions. Remember always to use the honorific with the first name only.

When addressing for example, Khun Tongchan's wife (or daughter), Prinya Jotiskasthira, say *Khun Prinya*, not Khun Prinya Jotikasthira. Use the wife's first name, not her husband's.

Thailand is a stratified society that has a monarchy and an honours system. Both are taken very seriously.

Address a female commoner appointed for reward by the King as *Khunying* (followed by first name). *Khunying* can only be used to address women, and is also used for inherited titles (see below).

A person with the title *Momluang* has inherited the title, and might be male or female. The correct oral form of address is to say the title followed by the first name. When familiarity is appropriate the use of *Khun* thereafter is permissible. The abbreviation M.L. is used in correspondence.

The father of a *Momluang* is a *Mom Rajawong*. It is a title showing Royal provenance. A woman can be a *Mom Rajawong* either by inheritance or by award, but a man can only be one by birth.

If a female *Mom Rajawong* marries a commoner, her children lose the title and are therefore addressed as *Khun*. If a male *Mom Rajawong* marries a commoner, the children become *Momluang*. If the parents were of equal rank before marriage, the children become *Mom Rajawong*. The oral form of address for a male *Mom Rajawong* is *Khunchai* (before the first name), but the abbreviation M.R. (followed by both names) is used in correspondence. For a woman, say *Khunying*, and abbreviate to M.R. (followed by both names) in correspondence.

Another Royal title is *Momchao*, whose holder can be male or female. The daughter of a Momchao is a *Mom Rajawong*. If the female Momchao marries a male commoner, she becomes a *Mom Rajawong*.

Note that the titles *Khunchai* and *Khunying* may also be used alone in conversation, as with "Which book do you recommend, Khunchai?"

Correspondence to a person with rank or position should mention the title. Address him/her as *Manager* or *President of Company x*, ending (when writing in English) with Yours Respectfully, though Yours Sincerely is acceptable.

In correspondence address a Minister as *Khun X, Minister of Y*. Orally, say *Than Ratthamontree*, or just *Than* ("you" in a respectful way). Don't follow this with the name.

Many forms of address apply to Buddhist religious leaders. The most useful to know are *Supreme Patriarch*, used alone as a reference to or upon introduction to the religious head, and *Phra* followed by first name, which is used when addressing ordinary monks.

Order of precedence for the 6 main tiers of the Royal family:

HM The King
His/Her Royal Highness, Prince/Princess
His/Her Highness, Prince/Princess
His/Her Serene Highness, Prince/Princess Mom Chao
Mom Rajawong
Momluang

Togo

Mademoiselle Yvone DIELADE

French is spoken and forms of address correspond to those used in France.

Mr = *Monsieur*   Mrs = *Madame*   Miss = *Mademoiselle*

Tonga

Mr Tevita' Otulau KOLOKIHAKAUFISI

There are 3 strata in Tongan society – commoners, nobles, and royalty.

When addressing ordinary citizens use the last name, which is the family name, applying UK forms of address. Thus: *Mr Tevita' Otulau KOLOKIHAKAUFISI.*

Wives adopt their husband's family name upon marriage. Unmarried women are addressed as Miss.

There are no special forms of address for those with professional qualifications.

There are 9 noblemen. A nobleman is a person who owns a village or island, and he is addressed by his one name, which is hereditary. This is not a surname, but a title. His wife is addressed as *Mrs* (plus noble name).

The Tongan royal family is granted the same courtesies by way of forms of address as would be the British royal family, save for some adjustments. The King is *His Majesty*, the eldest son is the *Crown Prince*, but the Prince uses his noble name because he owns land, and the children of royal children are all *Honourable*, whether male or female.

Trinidad & Tobago

Mr Clive Eric Morgan PEGUS

Forms of address correspond to those used in the UK.
Therefore: Mr John Brown and Mrs Mary Brown.

Some women retain their maiden name upon marriage by hyphenating it to their husband's name. Thus: *Mrs Mary Jones-Brown*.

Orally and in correspondence use Miss or Ms for unmarried women.

There are no hereditary titles and conferred titles are no longer awarded. However, medals are awarded for those with distinguished careers, and these persons should be addressed in correspondence by adding the initials of their award after the name.

Ministers should be addressed orally and in correspondence as Honourable Minister. Ambassadors are Your Excellency.

No distinction is made for persons with professional qualifications.

Tunisia

Sayeda (or Madame) AMEL Najet Mestiri

See also the chapter on Arab names.

The official language is Arabic but there is French influence, and you may use the usual French forms of address if you wish. Furthermore, many Tunisians, particularly students, speak English, German, or Italian as well.

When writing you should abbreviate Monsieur to *M.*, Mademoiselle to *Mlle*, and Madame to Mme. Note that *Mademoiselle*, in full, is seldom used.

In the vernacular:

Mr = *Sayed*   Mrs = *Sayeda*   Miss = *Anisa*

In general, in Tunisia you should not address someone by only their first name unless you are on familiar terms and you have been told it is all right to do so.

Within the string of Arab names everyone usually has their own given name followed by their father's given name. Complications arise as the string is added to by the practice of honouring ancestors.

There are no hard and fast rules with Arab names. Everything is loose and variable, and different influences will govern the practices of each Arab country.

The word sheikh, meaning "old man", is an honorific used among the tribes to describe a tribal leader or man of widely accepted distinction. It is not used as often in Tunisia as in the Gulf and other Middle Eastern countries.

Tunisia is different from other Arab countries in using Ben (son of) instead of bin, and by applying it liberally, as in the following example:

Example of the derivation of the name string of a male: Ali Ben Abdullah Ben Mughram Al-Ghamdi:

Given name	Father's name	Grandfather's name	Surname, perhaps tribal name
Ali *Ben*	Abdullah *Ben*	Mughram	Al-Ghamdi

Some surnames are derived from tribes as a matter of family tradition. The root name (i.e. the last name) is often a description of ancestors, a tribal name, or a place.

So you will tend always to find a person's given name and always the name of their father, frequently also their grandfather's name, then their tribal name, which often, but not always, is preceded by "Al".

In a further departure from Arab practice, women in Tunisia take their husband's name upon marriage.

In correspondence it is usual, but not the rule, to use the honorific followed by the given name, father's name, and last name. Therefore, if any names are to be left out, they should be those sandwiched between the father's name and the final name in the string. Thus: *Sayed Ali Ben Abdullah Al-Ghamdi.*

Titles are not as important in Tunisia as in most other Arab countries, and it is not customary to address people by their profession. Exceptionally, barristers are addressed as *Maître*, and doctors are addressed appropriately.

Turkey

ALI OSMAN Bey Anafarta

The family name is last, but see below.

In semi-formal conversation, and if you are meeting someone for business for the first time, you use the first names followed by *Bey* (for men), or *Hanım* (for women). Thus: Ali Osman Anafarta would be addressed as *Ali Osman Bey*.

In correspondence the order is reversed. Thus: *Bay Ali Osman Anafarta* (where Bey becomes Bay). However, women are addressed as *Bayan* instead of *Hanım*. Thus: *Bayan Aliye Osman Anafarta*.

You may also use *Sayın* (meaning Esquire) as a gender neutral oral or written form of address. It is followed by the family name. Thus: *Sayın Anafarta* (oral) or *Sayın Ali Osman Anafarta* (written).

The use of *Sayın* with *Bay* (or *Bayan*) adds prestige and esteem to written usage. Thus: *Sayın Bayan Aliye Osman Anafarta*.

There is no distinction between Miss and Mrs.

Women usually adopt their husband's family name upon marriage.

There are no hereditary or conferred titles.

The use of Efendi (m) and Hanımefendi (f)

"Efendi" is used after the first names as a polite form of address in certain circumstances, as with "*This is Ali Osman Efendi.*" Do not use it if you are introducing yourself, but when you introduce one party to another.

Following the establishment of the Republic in 1923 and the

abolition of the Ottoman titles a few years later, the word *Efendi* was discontinued for use as an official form of address. The word survived nonetheless and its application mutated over time. Previously, it was used to address someone of higher status. Today, it is used to the contrary for addressing someone who is lower in status than yourself. For instance, a householder introduces his elderly gardener as *Ali Osman Efendi*, or a landlady introduces her caretaker that way, or a provincial governor would call his porter that. (NB: Take care not to confuse *Efendi* with the similarly sounding *efendim*, which means "I beg your pardon".)

The feminine equivalent of Efendi is *Hanımefendi*, but it is very formal and is usually used when introducing or addressing highly respectable mature and elderly women, as with *Aliye Osman Hanımefendi*. Whilst the masculine form (Efendi) has lost status in time, Hanımefendi has suffered no such fate.

Turkmenistan

Whilst names are usually constructed in the Russian patronymic style, Russian honorifics are now seldom used, though they are well understood. Forms of address are experiencing gradual transition as Turkmen overtakes Russian custom.

IN TURKMEN:

Mr = Jenap   Mrs / Miss = Khanym

(But see below before using these honorifics.)

Note that *Khanym* is seldom used in everyday speech, and *Jenap* is a fairly recent innovation.

Unlike the other -*stan* countries, there is no Turkic influence on forms of address.

With a person's name string the forename comes first, then the patronymic which shows filiation to the father, then the surname, which is passed on down the generations. Thus:

Gylchmamet Orazovitch Orazov (m)

- For formal use, and if he holds a high position, he will be addressed by his first name + patronymic. Thus: *Gylchmamet Orazovitch*. The honorific *Jenap* should be used.
- Less formally, he may be orally addressed with the honorific and surname. Thus: *Jenap Orazov*.
- He may also be addressed without the honorific and in Turkmen style like this:
  Gylchmamet Oraz ogly Orazov, where *ogly* means "son of", and replaces the Russian patronymic (Oraz*ovitch*).
- Friends will call him by his first name. Thus: *Gylchmamet*.

Apply the same formulas with women, except *gyzy* (daughter of) is used instead of *ogly*. Thus: *Bibi Oraz gyzy Orazova*.

There is no distinction between married and unmarried women. Married women often take their husband's surname on marriage, but there is free choice and they do not necessarily do so.

Women are usually addressed without the honorific. Instead, an affinity word is placed after the first name. Which affinity to apply is determined not by one's kinship, but by one's familiarity with the person:

If the woman is older than you, she will be addressed as:
Ejeke (elder sister) after the firstname – used when one is quite close, OR
Gelneje (sister-in-law) after the firstname – used when very familiar, OR

Dayza (aunt) after the firstname – used generally and to older women, OR
Just use her firstname.

As a matter of course it is acceptable to address women by their first name only. Thus: *Bibi*. If her name is unknown, just say *Dayza*.

Similarly, men are often addressed as *Aga* (maternal elder brother) after firstname, OR
Dade (paternal elder brother) after firstname, OR
Dayi (uncle) after firstname

Male and female name structures tend to be transformed by prefixes and suffixes. With men these have general meanings but with women they usually are variations on words for loveliness.

For instance, *Mamet* (Mohammad) is frequently attached to a man's forename, either at the beginning or end, as with *Gylchmamet*, or *Mametgylch* – or to the patronymic, as with *Drazmamet* / *Mametoraz*.

A woman might attach *gul* (meaning Rose), thus *Bibigul*, or *Gulbibi* – or it might be attached to the patronymic, thus *Orazgul* / *Guloraz*.

Correspondence

With correspondence place *Hormatly* (respectable or honourable) before the first name, but use all names. Thus: *Hormatly Gylchmamet Orazovitch Orazov*. It is the same for men and women.

Use the honorific *Janap* only when writing to a high official. It may be placed before the surname or before the full name string. Otherwise, and for women, just use their names without the honorific. Open the letter by addressing them by their surname and firstname – but the envelope should be addressed to surname, patronymic, and firstname – in that order.

Men who have visited Mecca are addressed in speech and in writing as *Hajy* (before the firstname). There is no equivalent for women.

A mullah (Islamic teacher) is addressed as *Molla* (firstname), and a senior mullah is addressed as *Akhun* (firstname).

Turks & Caicos Islands

Mr Jude Bernard

Forms of address correspond to those used in the UK.

Tuvalu

Forms of address correspond to those used in the UK.

Uganda

Mr Donald Christian NYAKAIRU

Forms of address in Uganda are very much the same as for the UK with the business community.

Ukraine

Pan Mykola KRAVCHENKO

The Russsian patronymic pattern of surnames applies to the Ukraine, though to a lesser extent (see chapter on Russia). The use of patronymic names was introduced by Russia and is not a part of the Ukraine's historic tradition. They remain officially in use for identity cards, but for speech and writing people are now returning to their traditional forms of address.

Instead of Russian honorifics, use Polish:

Mr = *Pan*   Mrs = *Pani* (there is no equivalent for Miss).

In correspondence use the first initial followed by the family name. Thus *Sergii (Ivanovych) Ivanchuk* would be addressed as *S. Ivanchuk.*

United Arab Emirates
(of: Abu Dhabi, Dubai, Sharjah, Ajman,
Umm al Qaiwan, Ras al-Khaimah, Fujeira)

Sayyed Mohammed Abdullah ABDULRAHMAN

See also the chapter on Arab names, and the separate entry on Dubai.

Mr = *Sayyed*   Mrs = *Sayyiday*   Miss = *Anisah*

There are no hard and fast rules with Arab names. Everything is loose and variable, and different influences will govern the practices of each Arab country.

As a general term of address you may use the first name only, provided you are on familiar terms and you have been told to do so.

The name of Mohammed Abdullah Abdulrahman, an ordinary male citizen, is composed of the given name, father's name, and surname respectively. He should be addressed orally in formal circumstances as *Sayyed Abdulrahman*, but may be addressed as *Mohammed* in informal situations provided the circumstances described above apply.

Male friends will often address one another by inserting *Abu* (father of) before the family name, but foreign businessmen should not use this.

In correspondence, begin with *Dear Mr Abdulrahman* (formal), or *Dear Mohammed* (informal).

Apply the same formula for addressing in the UAE, whether orally or for correspondence. There is no hard and fast rule concerning a name change upon marriage. Generally, women retain their maiden names and in formal use, for passports, for instance, would be referred to as Mrs A, wife of B.

There are no conferred titles. The word Sheikh, meaning "old man", is an honorific used among the tribes to describe a tribal leader or man of widely accepted distinction. In the UAE, however, Sheikh applies to the rulers and leading members of the rulers' families.

The following forms of oral address apply:

The president of the UAE: Your Highness.

When speaking to an Emirati ruler, call him Your Highness, or, if speaking in Arabic it will be *Sumoukom*.

To a Sheikh: Your Excellency.
To a government Minister who is also a Sheikh: Your Excellency.

To other Ministers: Your Excellency.

Correct forms of address for correspondence:

To the President of the UAE: *His Highness, Sheikh* (add full name).

When writing to an Emirati Ruler, refer to him as *His Highness, Sheikh* (add full name), *Ruler of* (name of Emirate).

To a Sheikh: *His Excellency, Sheikh* (add full name).

To a government Minister who is also a Sheikh: *His Excellency, Sheikh* (add full name).

To other Ministers: *His Excellency, Sayyed* (add full name).

Example: *His Highness Sheikh Zayed Bin Sultan Al-Nahyan*, where *Zayed* is the first name, *Bin* means "son of", *Sultan* is the father's name, *Al-Nahyan* is the family name or last name.

In correspondence, when the Sheikh has a professional qualification:

H.H. Sheikh Dr Sultan Bin Mohammed Al-Qassimi

United Kingdom

Mr Lindsey SHANSON

For the benefit of foreign readers, a few words about basics:

Everyday citizens are addressed both orally and in writing by the conventional Mr, Mrs and Miss. People, whether male or female, are addressed in formal situations by their family name, which appears last. Thus: *Robert Harris* will be addressed as *Mr Harris*, and his wife will be *Mrs Harris*.

It used to be conventional to use first names only between people who know each other well, but tradition is changing, and the use of forenames without an honorific is now widespread even in business circles after an initial introduction. After you have been introduced to Mr Harris, whether for business or at a social function, he very likely would have no objection to being called *Robert* thereafter.

Increasingly, women are opting for the neutral *Ms* instead of *Miss* or *Mrs*, particularly in the workplace, and it is no longer a foregone conclusion whether a woman is married or single.

Contrary to practice in most other countries, British dentists have until now had to accept the honorific of the common man (or woman), and have therefore been addressed as plain *Mr*, *Miss*, or *Mrs*. That is changing.

The General Dental Council has now ruled that dentists may call themselves *Doctor* without it being deemed as professional misconduct.

Foreign dentists who visit the UK are nearly always addressed as *Doctor* because they retain their usual form of address whilst here, but British dentists going abroad, having adopted local custom and relished the short-lived experience, had to revert to type on their return. The change will now be entirely voluntary, so visitors should continue to address UK dentists plainly until such time as consumer resistance fades and the change is seen to be having an effect.

Another British idiosyncrasy concerns forms of address for members of the medical profession, though this extends to some Commonwealth countries too. A medical practitioner, like almost everywhere else, is addressed as Doctor, but a Fellow of the Royal College of Surgeons (who achieves this status long after qualifying as a doctor) reverts to being called Mr/Mrs/Miss (unless or until they acquire a PhD). Surgeons do, however, place the initials FRCS after their names, and these should be used in correspondence, but not for oral forms of address.

However, some traditions remain impervious to time. Those with an honour, whether hereditary or for their lifetime, will generally expect to be addressed appropriately, unless they ask you not to. Address a man with a knighthood or baronetcy as Sir followed by his given name only. For instance, address Sir Gilbert Harding as *Sir Gilbert* until he tells you to call him Gilbert. Never call him Harding. But address his wife as *Lady Harding*.

The custom is entirely different for Lords and Ladies. The BBC style guide recommends, for instance, that Lord Jeffrey Archer be addressed as *Lord Archer* because ennobled and titled men (other than those with a knighthood) are addressed by the title preceding their family name. But their wives are addressed by their full names on introduction, and by first name thereafter. Thus: *Lady Antonia Fraser* to begin with, then *Lady Antonia*. Never say *Lady Fraser*.

Marquesses, Earls, Viscounts, and Barons are all addressed orally as *Lord*, and their wives are addressed as *Lady*. A Baroness is a *Lady* in her own right. A Duke is always addressed as *Duke*, and a Duchess as *Duchess*. The daughter of a Duke, Marquess, or Earl, is a *Lady*. However, the first son of a Duke is a Marquess, but he is not a Peer (though this does not alter how to address him).

All peerages have a territorial base in their origin. (Thus: *Baron Smith of Bognor*). Except for those peerages which embrace a territory in their titles (whereupon their full name string should be used in formal situations), the territory does not form part of the title and it is not usual to use it in oral or written forms of address. Thus: *Baron Smith* is sufficient.

Courtesy titles, or titles connected with the family name of a Peer, usually affect only the descendants of that Peer. Life Peers rank with hereditary Barons and Baronesses according to the date of their creation. Wives of Peers, as stated, take the title of *Lady*, and the children are *The Honourable*. Husbands of female life Peers do not take a title. Children of female life Peers are *The Honourable*.

For a complete guide to correct forms of address concerning the titled and nobility of the United Kingdom we recommend that you refer to *Debrett's Correct Form*.

Constitutional Monarchies

It took only a moment to cover forms of address for ordinary citizens. For the extraordinary, there are many conventions. The following forms are recommended for constitutional monarchies.

THE QUEEN

Postal Address	Opening of letter	Introductions & oral address	Place cards
The Private Secretary to Her Majesty The Queen	Your Majesty	Your Majesty (subsequently Ma'am)	

THE QUEEN'S CHILDREN

His Royal Highness The Prince . . . etc	Your Royal Highness	Your Royal Highness (subsequently Sir/Madam)	

THE PRIME MINISTER

The Honourable* Mr Smith or Prime Minister	Honourable* Prime Minister or Dear Prime Minister	(The) Honourable* Prime Minister (Address:) Sir	The Prime Minister

*Canadian, UK, and other PMs who are Privy Councillors: Right Honourable

MINISTERS AND DEPUTY MINISTERS

The Honourable John Smith or Minister of . . .	Honourable Minister or Sir or Dear Minister	Honourable Minister or Sir or Minister	The Minister of . . .

THE SPEAKER

The Honourable John Smith	Mr Speaker or Honourable Speaker	Mr Speaker	The Speaker

THE CHIEF (OF) JUSTICE (in UK, address as Peer)

The Honourable John Smith	Honourable Chief Justice	(The) Honourable Chief Justice	The Chief Justice

THE LEADER OF THE OPPOSITION

The Honourable John Smith	Honourable Sir/Madam	The Honourable Sir/Madam	The Leader of the Opposition Party

MEMBERS OF PARLIAMENT

(The Honourable)* John Smith	Sir/Madam	Sir/Madam	Mr John Smith

* not in UK

AMBASSADORS AND HIGH COMMISSIONERS

His/Her Excellency	Your Excellency or Excellency	Your Excellency or Excellency	The Ambassador of ...

CHARGÉ D'AFFAIRES / ACTING HIGH COMMISSIONER

Mr/Mrs Smith	Sir/Madam	Sir/Madam	The Chargé d'Affaires of ...

ARCHBISHOPS

The Most Reverend (and Rt Hon.)* the Lord Archbishop of ...	Dear Archbishop	The Archbishop of ... Archbishop ...	His Grace, The Archbishop of ...

* Canterbury and York only

The Right Reverend Bishop of...	Dear Bishop	The Bishop of... Bishop...	The Bishop of...

THE CHIEF RABBI

The (Chief) Rabbi Dr...	Dear Chief Rabbi	Chief Rabbi	The Chief Rabbi

MEMBERS OF THE CIVIL SERVICE ARE ADDRESSED BY NAMES, NOT BY APPOINTMENTS, EXCEPT BY OTHER MEMBERS OF THEIR DEPARTMENTS.

FORMS OF ADDRESS USED FOR PRESIDENTS OF THE UNITED STATES (WHEN THEY ARE VISITING THE UK):

THE PRESIDENT OF THE UNITED STATES:

His Excellency Mr Smith, President of...	Your Excellency or Excellency or Mr President	Your Excellency or Excellency or Mr President	The President

THE PRESIDENT'S WIFE

Mrs Smith	Dear Mrs Smith	The First Lady, Mrs Smith Address: Ma'am	Mrs Smith

Republics

There is a distinction between the correct forms of address used by Republics and and those used by constitutional Monarchies. International convention is fairly uniform, though some countries may substitute their own customs. The following forms are recommended for dignataries visiting the UK from Republics.

Office	On envelope	Written salutation	Letter ending	Spoken	Invitation card
President	The President	(Dear) Mr President	I have the honour to be, Yours Faithfully	Mr President (subsequently: Mr President)	Invitations are extended by letter to the Private Secretary to the President, never by card
His wife	Mrs A. Smith	Dear Mrs Smith/ Madam	"	Mrs Smith/ Madam	"
The President & Wife	The President & Mrs A. Smith	(Dear) President & Mrs Smith	"	Mr President & Mrs Smith	"
Chief Justice	The Honourable Mr Justice Smith, Chief Justice of . . .	(Dear) Sir, or (Dear) Mr Chief Justice (& Mrs Smith)	"	Judge or Sir. In court: My Lord or Your Lordship	The Honourable The Chief Justice
Former President	Mr & Mrs A. Smith	Dear Mr (& Mrs) Smith	Yours faithfully	Sir/Mr Smith/ Madam	Mr & Mrs Smith
Cabinet Ministers	Mr A. Smith, MP, Minister of . . .	Dear Minister / Deputy Minister	"	Mr Minister / Deputy Minister, then Sir.	Mr A. Smith & Mrs Smith

(Note: For Mr substitute the correct title, e.g.: Dr; Prof.; Gen. etc.)

Speaker of Parliament	Mr A. Smith, MP, Speaker of Parliament	(Dear) Mr Speaker & Mrs Smith	"	Mr Speaker, then Sir.	"
Chairman of the President's Council	Mr A. Smith, Chairman of the President's Council	(Dear) Mr Chairman or (Dear) Sir	"	Mr Chairman, Sir then	"
Foreign Ambassador	His Excellency, Mr A. Smith	Your Excellency or Mr Ambassador or Dear Mr Ambassador & Mrs Smith	Official: Please accept, Your Excellency, /Mr Ambassador, the (renewed) assurance of my highest consideration Public: I have the honour to be, Yours faithfully	Your Excellency, or, Mr Ambassador / Sir Wife: Mrs Smith / Madam	The Ambassador of ... & Mrs A. Smith
Mayor/Mayoress	His/Her Worship, The Mayor/ Mayoress of ...	Dear Mr Mayor/ Madam Mayoress	Yours faithfully	Mr Mayor/ Madam Mayoress, then Sir/Madam	

Note: The Ambassador of one's own country is not addressed as Excellency / Mr Ambassador / Sir. Mr Smith is correct.

Note: When an envelope is addressed to a person in office, the spouse is not included on the envelope even if the letter or card includes the spouse.

United States of America

Mr Raymond G. MORRISON

There are several important differences from the forms of address used in the UK. For instance, in the United States administration they have *Secretaries*, not *Ministers*. Someone who is a Minister in America holds a religious office. Here are some other distinctions:

Esquire (or Esq.) is very rarely used in the British way. Esquire is, however used for lawyers, male or female.

In the South, many youngsters are taught to address their elders as Sir or Madam rather than using the elder's name.

Junior:

The use of the suffix Junior is a particularly American custom, and its use sometimes causes confusion. It applies only to the male line.

A man with exactly the same name(s) as his father uses *Junior* after his name as long as his father remains alive. Thus: *John (Cuthbert) Doe Junior.* He may drop it after his father dies, but that is optional. Generally, men tend to retain it for a few years then drop it.

If Junior has a son and gives him his own name(s), the son becomes *John (Cuthbert) Doe 3rd* (so long as his grandfather remains alive and his father remains Junior).

A male might also be named after an uncle, grandfather, or cousin, and he will then be addressed as *John Cuthbert Doe 2nd.*

A wife retains the same suffix after her name as her husband. Thus: *Mrs John Cuthbert Doe 3rd.*

Some family names are carried on for several generations, so difficulties arise when someone in the chain dies. There is no ready rule for this; sometimes everyone moves up one notch, sometimes not – because people become known in society by their suffix and confusion follows a change.

When the parents of *John Cuthbert Doe 2nd* reside in the same city, they usually take on the suffix *Senior* to avoid confusion, particularly between the mother and her daughter-in-law. This is expressed in writing as *Sr.*

In correspondence the practise is to write to *John Cuthbert Doe jr.* (where *Junior* is expressed in lower case with a period). However, the envelope should be addressed to *John Cuthbert Doe Jr.*

Authorities differ on the correct written utilisation of the suffix. Some maintain that it should be expressed as a Roman numeral (thus: John Cuthbert Doe III), others that it should not (as with John Cuthbert Doe 3rd). We regard it as optional.

Professional qualifications

Professor: the term is regarded by some as old fashioned. Note that, unlike the UK custom, any university teacher is usually called *Professor*.

Doctor of Medicine: Say "Doctor", but write to John K. Smith, M.D. Also use Doctor for surgeons, dentists, and vets.

The courtesy title Honourable is used officially by the following when they are addressed by name:

American Ambassadors
American Secretaries (including those with personal rank)
American Representatives in International Organisations.
Deputy & Assistant Heads of Indep Gvt Agencies.
Asstnt Secs of Exec Depts & Officers of comparable rank.
Assistants & Special Assistants to the President.

Boards, members of equal rank.
Cabinet Officers.
Commissioners.
Foreign Ministers.
Governors of States & Territories.
Heads of Major organisations within the Federal Agencies
High Officers of State Gvts.
Judges (but not Justices of the Supreme Court).
Legal Advisers & Officers of comparable rank.
Mayors of Cities
Senators
State Cabinet & Legislative Officials.
Under Secs & Officers of comparable rank of Executive Depts.
US Representatives of International Organisations

Consuls, but Not Honorary Consuls, are given the courtesy title of Honorable in official correspondence.

When writing, place "The Honorable" on the first line of the envelope. The title is not used in conjunction with prefixes such as Mr, or Mrs, rank, or academic degree, e.g. *The Honorable John Smith*. More informally, it may be abbreviated to "The Hon." before the name.

"The Hon." is not used in issuing or answering invitations.

His/Her Excellency is the usual social form for State Governors, Ambassadors. It is usual to write His/Her Excellency on the line above the name. More informally it may be abbrev to H.E.

Open a letter with: My dear Mr/Madam Ambassador
Close a letter with:

Social: Respectfully yours, or Sincerely yours.
Business: Very truly yours

American Ambassadors accredited to countries in Central and South

America are never referred to as The American Ambassador, but as *The Ambassador of the United States*.

Wives of Ambassadors are not accorded any special style.

Verbal address of Ambassador: *Mr/Madam Ambassador* (followed by name – optional), or *Your Excellency*.

When addressing foreign ambassadors resident in Washington:

Beginning of letter:

Yr Excellency

Closing with:

Social: Sincerely yours
Business: Very truly yours

Envelope:

His Excellency
Full name
The Ambassador of . . .

Joint form of address: *His Excellency, The Ambassador of . . ., and Mrs (Surname).*

Footnote

Federal custom bestows the title *The Honorable* by courtesy for life on the President, Vice President, Senators, Congressmen, Governors, Cabinet Members, and all Federal Judges, Ministers Plenipotentiary, and (American) Ambassadors. A Senator continues to be addressed as *Senator* (before family name), even when no longer in office.

Do not use these titles as a general oral form of address (except for Senators).

They are never used on stationery by the person who holds or held office, so they do not appear on letterheads or visiting cards. They are used only for formal oral introduction, and on formal invitations and business letters addressed to that personality, abbreviating to either *The Hon.* or *Hon.* (followed by names). In such correspondence use *The Honorable* before the full name string (never directly before the surname), and do not capitalise the definite article when used in the text of correspondence (so that *The Hon John Doe* as a title becomes *the Honorable John Doe* in third party reference).

The wives of officials, from the President down, are not entitled to a courtesy title and should be addressed as if they are ordinary citizens. The President's wife is addressed as The First Lady, Mrs Clinton (without first name), or just as Mrs Clinton. However, the wives of officials below the President are addressed with forenames and surname.

When it is the husband who is the spouse of a title-holder, he does not share her title and is addressed in the usual way for an ordinary person.

Although it is correct to speak to Mr President; Mr / Madam Secretary (of State); Mr/Mrs Ambassador; Mr/Mrs Mayor – say Governor (not Mr Governor) and say Congressman / Congresswoman (not Mr Congressman, etc).

Uruguay

Señor Leonel Ricardo ENRIQUE Macial

See also the general chapters on Spanish American forms of address

SPANISH IS SPOKEN.

Orally:

Mr = *Señor*   Mrs = *Señora*   Miss = *Señorita*

In correspondence abbreviate to:

Sr.   *Sra.*   *Srta.*

People usually have two given names followed by their father's surname, then their mother's surname.

Unlike most other Latin-American countries, one still refers to the father's and mother's family names in informal correspondence.

When *Señor Pérez* marries *Señorita María Valdez*, she keeps her name and acquires her husband's surname. Thus: *Señora María Valdez de Pérez*. A child called Pedro would be *Pedro Pérez Valdez*, with the father's family name preceding the mother's.

In correspondence, women retain the preposition de (of) before the husband's name. Thus *María Valdez de Pérez*. If they divorce, she reverts to her maiden name.

There are no conferred or hereditary titles.

Persons with rank or position are addressed simply as *Señor* or *Señora* followed by the rank. Thus *Señor* Ministro, *Señora* Embajadora, *Señor* General.

Professional titles such as Ingeniero or Licenciado are not generally used conversationally except as a solitary salutation. Thus "Good morning, Licenciado".

For professional people, these written forms of address are appropriate, where the honorific (Señor etc) is followed by the courtesy title then the person's given name(s) and surname(s). Thus:

Licenciado/a – for someone with a degree in humanities.
Ingeniero – for someone with a degree in engineering.
Doctor/a – for someone with a doctorate.

EXAMPLE: *Señor Lic. Vicente Morales.*

When writing, these titles are usually shortened to Lic., Ing., Dr./Dra. Note that Dr./Dra. are very often used as courtesy titles.

Uzbekistan

Gospodin Mahmoud AHMEDOV Rasulovich

A change in direction from the traditional use of the patronymic system as used in Russia is now evident, though in formal circumstances it is still chiefly used. About 87% of the population is Muslim & Turkic, Russian 8%, and other 5%.

When adopting Russian honorifics:

Mr = *Gospodin*   Mrs/Miss = *Gospozha*

There is no distinction between married and unmarried women.

The forename comes first, then the surname, then the patronymic which shows filiation to the father. Thus: Mahmoud Ahmedov Rasulovich would be addressed as *Mahmoud Ahmedov*, or *Gospodin Ahmedov*, and his wife would be *Gospozha Ahmedova*.

In the above example, *Mahmoud* is the given name, *Ahmedov* is the surname, and *Rasulovich* is the patronymic. The patronymic is formed by adding "son of" or "daughter of" to the father's name. See the chapter on Russia for more details.

Changes in forms of address are taking place slowly, with Uzbek forms replacing the Russian patronymic.
Alisher Faizullaef Rasulovich (m) would become, in his new guise, *Alisher Faizulla ogli* (where *ogli* means son of). Similarly, his wife would be *Gullora* Faizullaefa kizi (f) (where *kizi* means daughter of).

In Uzbek:

Mr = *Janob*   Mrs / Miss = *Honim*

Therefore write to, or say: *Janob Alisher* or *Honim Gullora* (though in writing use the full name string).

Sometimes men are addressed by placing the word *Bek* (meaning Sir) after the first name. It is a hereditary title passed down the male line. Thus: *Mahmoud Bek*. In general this is used by the gentry and moneyed classes; and is adopted in official documents, such as passports.

Male Muslims who have visited Mecca place *Haja* before their names. Women use *Haji*.

Vanuatu

Master Paul TELUKLUK

The community speaks English or French, but not necessarily both. Identify which community you are addressing, then use either French or English forms of address, as appropriate.

The binding language is Bislama, which both communities speak. It is a form of pidgin that has oral forms of address which are not normally expressed in writing.

IN BISLAMA:

Mr = *Master*   Miss & Mrs = *Missis*

Women are commonly addressed by their names, without the honorific.

Missis is used in moderation, because one often refers to women by reference to male relatives. An example of the opposite is how Prince Charles was addressed – he was called *Pikinini Belong Kween*.

In English:

Mr   Mrs

In French:

Mr = *Monsieur*   Mrs = *Madame*   Miss = *Mademoiselle*

In all three languages the honorific precedes the last name (family name).

Vatican State

We are advised that the official language is Latin, but correspondence may be addressed in whatever language you wish. In practice this should be in Italian, English, French, German, or Spanish.

In Latin:

Mr = *Dominus* (or Domine if addressing someone directly)
Mrs = *Domina*   There is no form of address for an unmarried
woman.

Latin forms might well be used between some members of the community in the State, but its use by a lay person would be somewhat eccentric.

Refer to *Debrett's Correct Form* for correct Catholic ecclesiastical forms of address.

Venezuela

Señor Alfonso José MONTES Álvarez

See also the general entry on Spanish American forms of address.

SPANISH IS SPOKEN.

Orally:

Mr = *Señor*   Mrs = *Señora*   Miss = *Señorita*

In correspondence abbreviate to:

Sr.   *Sra.*   *Srta.*

People usually have two given names followed by their father's surname, then their mother's surname.

Often, for informal greetings, the second given name and/or the mother's surname, are dropped. Thus, *Juan Antonio Castillo Salazar* might be known as *Juan Castillo Salazar*, *Juan Antonio Castillo*, or simply *Juan Castillo*.

Married women replace their mother's surname with that of their husband, preceded by the preposition de (of). Thus *María González Quintero* would become *María González de Castillo*.

Never use *don* or *doña*.

There are no conferred or hereditary titles.

Address persons with rank as *Señor* or *Señora* followed by the rank. Thus *Señor Ministro*, *Señora Embajadora*, *Señor General*.

For persons with professional titles, the oral form of address is appropriate, followed by the person's given name(s) and surname(s). The titles are:

> *Licendiado/a* – for someone with a degree in humanities.
> *Ingeniero/a* – for someone with a degree in engineering.
> *Doctor/a* – for someone with a doctorate.

Thus: *Licenciado Vicente Morales.*

Note that Doctor(a) is a general term of respect that is widely used for educated people.

Whether writing or speaking, do not use the honorific with the courtesy title (thus Señor Licenciado . . . is wrong)

When writing, these titles may be shortened to Lic., Ing., Dr./Dra.

Vietnam

Mr Chau Tran PHONG

In Vietnamese, no single set of honorifics exists. Instead, people identify themselves (as well as others) using family terms that depend on relative age and familiarity. Everybody, related or not, becomes a *sister* or *brother*, *uncle* or *aunt*.

The first name is the family name, but the usual custom is to address people by their given name (last name). Even friends will use the last name on its own. Sometimes, usually when there are many others with the same name, people also use their middle name to avoid confusion.

Nguyẻn is a very popular family name; so popular that some Westerners mistake it for an honorific. It is not.

Married women retain their family name, and children will have their father's family name.

When writing, men insert the joining-word *Van*, and women use

Thi between the first and last name. Thus: Đặng *văn* Thu. Văn and Đặng *thị* Thúy Vyên. Văn and Thị have no particular meaning as a form of address (though in conversation they have many meanings, such as *fruit, river*, etc).

In conversation you should use only the last name. Some families use double, or compound names. Thus: with *Thúy-Vyên* say both names.

Members of People's Committees are addressed orally and in writing as *Vy Ban* (pronounced "we ban"), which means "committed person". Thus (when writing): *Vy Ban Đặng văn Thu*. Men may also be referred to as *Qui Ong* (gentleman of the Committee).

Virgin Islands (British)

Forms of address correspond to those used in the UK.

Virgin Islands (of the United States)

Mrs Marilyn STAPLETON

The island group exhibits a mixture of American customs strongly flavoured by Hispanic traditions. English is the official language, though Spanish and Creole are also widely spoken.

American forms of address are widely accepted in business circles.

In general, use American English. Otherwise you may employ Spanish forms:

Use the following before the last name.

Mr = *Señor*   Mrs = *Señora*   Miss = *Señorita*

In correspondence abbreviate to:

Sr.   *Sra.*   *Srta.*

Wallis & Fortuna

French forms of address should be used in the same way as in France.

Mr = *Monsieur*   Mrs = *Madame*   Miss = *Mademoiselle*

Western Sahara

Forms of address correspond largely to those used in Morocco.

The official language is Arabic but French is widely spoken.

Mr = *Sayed*   Miss / Mrs = *Lalla*

Use the honorific before the family name (see below).

However, *Sayed* may be abbreviated to *Si*, and is used in this form before either the family name, or, with more familiarity, before the given names. Thus: Sayed *BENNIS Abdel-Ilah*: *Si Bennis*, or *Si Abdel-Ilah*.

Women use *Lalla* before the given name, not the family name.

Always use the honorific until familiarity is sufficiently obvious for the use of the given names to be mutually acceptable. This will not take long to achieve.

Family names exist and usually appear first in the name string. The name string ordinarily comprises just two names, which, unlike in the Gulf countries, are not connected by the use of *bin* or *al* (son of). The exception is when the Prophet's name is given to males, which will appear first (as Mohammad) in the string but is rarely mentioned when addressing someone.

Hyphenated names, as with *Abdel-Ilah* in the above example, are held to be one name.

Women usually retain their maiden names after marriage. Official documents, such as passports, give their names, followed by the entry *spouse of . . .*

There are no particular forms of address for persons with professions.

Spain, Mauritania, and Morocco have all been involved in colonising the territory. Spanish and English are widely understood, though French forms of address are the natural alternative to Arabic.

Use:

Monsieur   Madame   Mademoiselle

Oral and written forms are the same except that instead of Mademoiselle use the abbreviation *Melle.*

In correspondence the family name appears first, followed by given name(s). Thus: *Monsieur HAMDAN Hassan*, where Hamdan is the family name. Similarly, it will be *Madame Hamdan* and *Melle. Hamdan* (Miss).

Formal invitations are addressed to Monsieur/Madame *Family Name* then *Given Name*.

However, the order is reversed for oral communication. A businessman meeting someone for the first time would use both names, then say Monsieur HASSAN on subsequent meetings. Colleagues tend to say both names (given name then family name). Government officials, for instance, always address one another by their given name then family name.

References to someone in the third person are by saying the given name then family name.

See the chapter on Morocco for more information.

Western Samoa and American Samoa

Mr Afamasaga Faamatala TOLEAFOA

In Western Samoa, forms of address correspond to those used in the UK. When using English say Mr/Mrs/Miss Lastname.

When writing formally, use all names. Informally, you may use the surname preceded by the initials as in the UK.

Women adopt their husband's family name upon marriage.

Dignitaries, those with honours, and Chiefs, should be addressed in Samoan.

Dignitaries are addressed with a formal and politely intoned "Your Excellency", which in Samoan is *Lau Afioga*. When formally welcoming a Chief the custom is to say *Afio Mai* (welcome) *Lau Afioga* followed by his chiefly title. For a simple introduction, as distinct from a welcoming, omit the *Afio Mai*.

American Samoa is influenced more by American custom, and American forms of address apply. Otherwise forms of address are much the same as for Western Samoa, with Chiefs and dignitaries addressed in Samoan, as above.

Yemen

Sayed HADI Ali Abdullah Abo-Lohom

See also the chapter on Arab names.

Mr = *Sayed*   Mrs = *Sayeda*   Miss = *A'nisa*

Some names are derived from tribes as a matter of family tradition. The root name (i.e. the last name) is often a description of ancestors, a tribal name, or a place.

Women retain their maiden name upon marriage and there is often no way to distinguish between a married and unmarried woman by her name. When writing to a married woman the custom is to address it to the "family of..." followed by the husband's family name.

There are no hard and fast rules with Arab names. Everything is loose and variable, and different influences will govern the practices of each Arab country.

Within the string of Arab names everyone usually has their own given name followed by their father's given name. Thus: Mohamad Jemal or Mohamad bin Jemal. Complications arise as the string is added to by the practice of honouring ancestors.

The word sheikh, meaning "old man", is an honorific used among the tribes to describe a tribal leader or man of widely accepted distinction.

Example of the derivation of the name string of a man, Ali Abdullah Mughram Al Ghamdi:

Given name	Father's name	Grandfather's name	Surname, perhaps tribal name
Ali	Abdullah	Mughram	Al-Ghamdi

In correspondence it is usual, but not the rule, to use the honorific followed by the given name, father's name, and last name. Therefore, if any names are to be left out, they should be those sandwiched between the father's name and the final name in the string.

Titles are important. When corresponding address people by their qualifications. Thus an engineer will be *Engineer Ali-Ghamdi*. This applies to most professions, though there is no firm rule. Military titles are particularly important and should always be used.

In oral address too, use the professional title. On subsequent mention one should say simply "Engineer", or "Doctor", etc.

So you will tend always to find a person's given name and always the name of their father, frequently also their grandfather's name, then their tribal-type name, which often, but not always, is preceded by "Al".

The same principle applies to men and to women.

People generally do not call someone only by their first names except between close social friends. They will always use the honorific before the given name when addressing each other at work. Thus, using the example of the name string above, he would be addressed simply as *Mr Ali*.

However, you may use the first name only provided you are on familiar terms and you have been told to do so.

In correspondence it is usual, but not the rule, to use the honorific followed by the given name, father's name, and last name. Thus: *Sayed Ali Abdullah Al-Ghamdi*. Therefore, if any names are to be left out, they should be those sandwiched between the father's name and the final name in the string.

In our example, the Al-Ghamdi will be carried forward to the next generation so will always remain the final name in the string.

Yugoslavia (Serbia and Montenegro)

Gospodine Radomire JERGICU

The given name always appears first, followed by the family name(s). Married women who have retained their maiden name add it to their husband's family name.

Some French and English influence affects forms of address. However, when addressing ordinary people, follow these rules:

Orally, address people as:

    Mr = *Gospodine*   Mrs = *Gospodjo*   Miss = *Gospodjice*

When writing, use the same spelling in the correspondence, but change to the following for the envelope (as third person):

    Mr = *Gospodin*   Mrs = *Gospodja*   Miss = *Gospodjica*

The following abbreviations are acceptable for all correspondence:

    Mr = *Gdin*   *Mrs = Gdja*   Miss = *Gdjica*

Someone with a Master's degree is addressed as *Magistre*. Use *Doktore* for a person with a medical qualification or PhD. Someone with a degree in engineering should be addressed in writing as Ing. Thus: *Ing. Rancic Dragan*.

There are no hereditary titles.

When writing formally to an ordinary citizen, open the letter with "Postovani gospidine" (followed by the family name), and close it with "S postovanjem" before signing off.

Person of rank, such as Ministers, Ambassadors, etc. are addressed orally as *Gospodine ambasadore*, or as *Ekselencija*. In writing, use *G. ministar*, or *Njegova Ekselencijo Ambassador*.

Zaïre

Monsieur IWULA Nsangolo

French is the national language, and forms of address correspond to those used in France. Thus:

Mr = *Monsieur*   Mrs = *Madame*   Miss = *Mademoiselle*

However, when addressing people by their surname, note that it appears first in the name string. Thus: Iwula Nsangolo would be *Monsieur Iwula*. Amongst friends he would be *Nsangolo*.

Women retain their maiden names upon marriage, though in formal documents, such as passports, it would say "wife of . . ."

Children adopt the father's family name.

There are tribal titles, but with more than 250 dialects and just as many customs we shall forego recording them all.

Zambia

Mr Mukaya MUKANGA

Forms of address in Zambia are the same as for the UK.

Zimbabwe

Miss Sekayi Jessica PSWARAYI

English is the first language for business, so use the forms of address that apply to the UK.

There are tribal titles, but they are in local dialects and foreigners would not be expected to use them.

Women adopt their husband's family name upon marriage.

There are no special forms of address for persons with academic qualifications.

Ex-ambassadors retain their title after retiring.